What People ar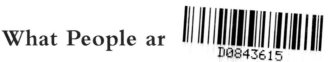

D0843615

FORGIVENESS:
The Mystery and Miracle

Finding Freedom and Peace At Last

"*Forgiveness: The Mystery and Miracle* is a gift to us all since no one avoids the reality of needing to deal with forgiveness, including the challenging reality of forgiving ourselves. To open her heart and soul to the world is an act of courageous vulnerability, and in dong so, Annette Stanwick has outlined a blueprint for living with power and passion, regardless of any pain that has become part of our life journey. Anyone who takes the message of this book to heart will also be released to find the freedom, peace and power that God ultimately wants for us all."

Bill Spangler, Marketing Director,
CHOICES Unlimited Seminars

"Annette Stanwick invites readers to walk with her on a journey from devastation and anger to healing and forgiveness in the wake of trying to cope with the murder of her brother. Her purpose is not merely to share her story but to offer others a way to deal with tragedy and injustice that follows the example of Jesus of Nazareth."

Warren C. Trenchard, Ph.D., Provost, La Sierra University

"It is my experience as a Professional Therapist that until the emotion of grief (due to losses in life), is expressed and worked through, individual hearts cannot be open to experiencing the joys and satisfactions of life. Forgiveness is the key aspect of this healing process.

In *Forgiveness: The Mystery and Miracle,* Annette Stanwick bares the deep woundedness of her heart to us. She highlights how her choice to forgive as Jesus forgave and taught, leads her to freedom and love, and away from remaining stuck in woundedness. This book will inspire the reader to consider Annette's practical suggestions to transformation and new life. It will bring renewed hope to all who seek healing."

Marilyn K. Smelski, Ph. D., R.S.W.
Registered Social Worker in Clinical Private Practice

"*Forgiveness: The Mystery and Miracle* reveals the resiliency of the human spirit and how positive choices can lead to freedom and peace in spite of the agonizing reality of disappointment and pain. Through the powerful personal quest for healing, and the model Annette Stanwick shares in this book, we are encouraged to seek healing from our own wounds.

This book encourages us to face challenges head on, determining not to allow the struggles of life to embitter, but rather to focus on letting go of those things that bind our hearts. This book will help you focus on finding your way through the obstacles on your path."

Fran Hewitt, Internationally acclaimed workshop facilitator
and Co-author of bestseller, *The Power of Focus for Women*

"In *Forgiveness: The Mystery and Miracle* an anguished soul opens to us as Annette Stanwick shares her story of family losses, intensified by the horrific murder of her dear brother Soren.

We are privileged to learn from a spiritual journey that demanded the full expression of her woundedness in an effort to move towards the forgiveness of her brother's murderer that set her free to love deeply again.

Her story of profound suffering leads all of us to realize our need for courage, honesty, prayer, forgiveness and ultimately God."

Rev. Bob Glasgow, Calgary Health Region,
Grief Support Program Coordinator

"A gift to humanity! The world needs this book to guide us ever upward in the spiral dance of healing. The author's pristine transparent voice carries the painful story shared by too many families who have lost loved ones to murder. It carries a message of hope to all who have abruptly found themselves belonging to a club for which they had not signed up.

Forgiveness: The Mystery and the Miracle invites the reader to process experiences of loss through questioning and prayer. A welcomed uplifting companion to those who are ready for the journey—the freeing journey of forgiveness!"

Lucille Mandin, Ph.D., University of Alberta

FORGIVENESS:
The Mystery and Miracle

Finding Freedom and Peace at Last

FORGIVENESS: The Mystery and Miracle
Finding Freedom and Peace at Last

Copyright © 2007 Annette Stanwick

The information in the Personal Application and Exploration sections of *Forgiveness: The Mystery and Miracle,* is for information purposes only. It is not intended to substitute for professional advice and counseling.

All scripture quotations are from *The Holy Bible, New Living Translation,* Copyright 1997 by Tyndale House Publishers Inc.

FIRST EDITION

Printed in Canada

Publisher: **Heart Message Publishing**
6620 62nd Avenue N.W.
Calgary, Alberta, Can. T3B 3E8
heartmessage@shaw.ca / www.annettestanwick.com

Library and Archives Canada Cataloging in Publication

Stanwick, Annette, 1944-
    Forgiveness: the mystery and miracle: finding freedom and peace at last
    / Annette Stanwick; editors, Rod Chapman & Elissa Oman.

    Includes bibliographical references and index.
    ISBN 978-0-9783545-0-3

    1. Forgiveness. I. Chapman, Rod, 1953- II. Oman, Elissa III. Title.

BF637.F67S83 2007   155.9'2   C2007-903016-5

EDITING:
Rod Chapman, ParisSojourn@gmail.com
Elissa Collins Oman, eco@editors.ca

COVER/BOOK DESIGN & LAYOUT:
Ghaile Pocock, Bulldog Communication Inc., bulldogcom@shaw.ca

PHOTOGRAPHY:
Author Photograph, Julie Jenkins; Memorial Photograph, Carol Lebrecht

PRINTING:
Friesen Printers, 120, 3016 - 19th St. N.E., Calgary, AB Canada T2E 6Y9

FORGIVENESS:
The Mystery and Miracle

Finding Freedom and Peace at Last

ANNETTE
STANWICK

HEART MESSAGE
PUBLISHING

First Edition
Calgary, Alberta

In Loving Memory of Soren Cornforth
1949 – 1999

DEDICATION

I DEDICATE THIS BOOK to the life, legacy and memory of my precious brother, Soren Cornforth. His death due to violence started me down an incredible path where my heart was miraculously healed and my life was utterly transformed.

TRIBUTE

TO GOD BE THE GLORY for the things he has done. Through forgiveness he has healed, restored and renewed my life, my heart and my soul. He has given me inspiration, passion, direction and strength along with the support of a wonderful team that has enabled me to bring this message to you—a message that comes from the depths of my heart.

DESIRE

IT IS MY HEARTFELT DESIRE that you, my readers, will be inspired to seek healing, freedom and peace in your own lives despite the difficult circumstances you encounter along life's journey.

ACKNOWLEDGEMENTS

I NEVER REALIZED HOW MANY PEOPLE would be so important in making my book dream a reality. I have truly been blessed by many wonderful people working behind the scenes—coaching, guiding, encouraging, cheering and providing assistance in countless meaningful ways.

To my beloved husband Clay, I can't begin to express my heartfelt appreciation for your unconditional love, encouragement, understanding and tangible day-to-day support. Every step of the way through some tough life experiences you stayed close beside me. Your tireless efforts helped me find a way to make this book possible.

To my beautiful daughters, Mona Dury and Shelann McQuay, along with Shelann's husband Barry, and my precious grand-children Orlando, Shea and Breanne McQuay, I love you all so much. Your support and love have been unbelievably wonderful.

To my amazing brothers, Chris and Rick Cornforth, I say thank you for the fun, enthusiasm, strength, courage, acceptance and love you role modeled as we journeyed life together.

Les and Fran Hewitt, you are the spark that set the wheels in motion for this book. Your vast experience, focus, ideas, coaching and gentle prodding have kept me going when I was tired and discouraged.

Dr. Jaelene Mannerfeldt and Jim Jenkins, your fabulous mountain chalet provided the space, solitude and a spectacular view that inspired me to go deep in thought, putting the messages from my heart into my writing.

To Glenn Gimbel, I say thank you for your professional wisdom, listening ear and for allowing me the freedom to balance my responsibilities in order to finish this project.

To the members of my writing group, I convey my sincere gratitude for your patience, your incredible encouragement and your insightful comments as I processed many of life's experiences through our times of writing together. In those memorable times, I dared start down the path toward seeing my thoughts bound in the pages of a book.

To Dr. Marilyn K. Smelski, your professional insights and perspectives regarding the healing process are absolutely invaluable.

Carl Belyea, your wonderful sculpture David was a powerful inspiration and illustration for an important chapter in this book.

Cathy Meyer-Nielson, your heart and your computer skills are awesome.

Thank you could never possibly be enough for my panel of readers—Clay Stanwick, Deanna Nygaard, Dianne Federation, Elissa Oman, Ghaile Pocock, Dr. Jaelene Mannerfeldt, Nancy Cowtun, Sarah Drew and Wayne Federation. Your candid thoughts, observations and opinions have truly made me a better writer. I could never have done it without your input.

Georgina Forrest, your organization, ideas and process were amazing. Thank you for your patience with me.

Ghaile Pocock, I can't begin to say how much I appreciate your artistic abilities in creating the cover and internal feel of my book. Your creativity, process and questions have inspired me to think, dream and plan. Rod Chapman and Elissa Collins Oman, your editorial skills are inimitable! You've blessed me beyond words.

Julie Jenkins, your photographic skill is captivating and I am so grateful you were the one to take my portrait.

Carol Lebrecht, your photographic artistry has memorialized the essence and personality of my precious brother Soren.

Darlene West, your eye for detail and your prayerful presence have been such a blessing.

Glenda Mason, you've traveled with me all the way with your words, your heart and your creativity.

FOREWORD

PEOPLE EVERYWHERE ARE SEARCHING for peace and freedom along with joy, satisfaction and happiness in their lives. In working with thousands of individuals over several decades of CHOICES Seminars, I have come to realize the deep needs people have in finding their way through difficult times.

In keeping with my personal commitment to transform lives… One heart at a time, I sense the book *Forgiveness: The Mystery and Miracle* has the potential to transform hearts and lives through the power of personal choice and forgiveness.

Annette Stanwick's magnetic vulnerability, candor and human-ness in sharing her own personal tragedies helps one sense her sincere desire to aid others in finding freedom and peace in spite of their difficulties. This book is more than just a spectacular story. The transition from the compelling narrative in each chapter to a personal application for each reader gives this book a unique quality that helps one feel they have just found a new friend who wants to help them through their own life struggles.

Annette's personal experiences are amazing. Her insights are remarkable, and her ability to find deep learning and healing in spite of the tragedies she has faced, gives the reader hope that they too can endure, overcome and rise above their own unique circumstances. Individuals cannot heal from those things they do not acknowledge. Throughout *Forgiveness: The Mystery and Miracle,* Annette has clearly created a path that gently helps the reader acknowledge the circumstances that prevent them from experiencing joy, love and satisfaction in their lives. She then helps them find a way to let go of those things that bind and hold one back from experiencing the freedom and peace they seek.

This book is a powerful portrayal of deep faith, human courage and triumph over tragedy that is miraculously transformed into a passion for helping others. The power of choice and the miracle of forgiveness revealed in this book have the potential to bring healing to individuals from all walks of life, from all types of wounds and from every corner of the globe.

It is Annette's deep desire that in reading this book, the subtitle, *Finding Freedom and Peace at Last* will be your personal experience in the journey of healing.

This book is a must-read. When you pick it up you won't want to lay it down.

Thelma Box
Founder and President
CHOICES Seminars

CONTENTS

INTRODUCTION

WE ALL ENCOUNTER PAINFUL SITUATIONS in our lives, and they affect us all in different ways. We respond to these situations differently depending on our perspectives—our beliefs, experience, knowledge and understanding of the world. How we deal with painful situations determines if we move on in life, or remain stuck in the aftermath of the crisis.

Our lives are defined not by the worst things that happen to us. We are defined by what we choose to do with the bad things that happen. We are defined by the choices we make in response to crisis. This book is about a major crisis in my life. It was the most difficult situation I have ever encountered. The book is about how I reacted to it, and how I dealt with it.

When I started writing, I felt like an artist standing before an empty canvas wondering where to put the first brush stroke. How could I possibly capture the enormity of the experiences that now define me, that now underline everything about who I am, what I do and how I view life?

As I began to describe my incredible journey, I came to realize that my purpose in writing is to help others understand the powerful influence of personal choice and the miracle of forgiveness. I hope others will benefit and even grow from the naked truth of my story, from hearing about the decisions I made not to allow grief, anger and resentment to overtake me, despite the pain. The journey through healing from a painful experience can be challenging, but the rewards are worth the effort. In sharing my personal crisis and the obstacles I faced, along with the experiences that helped me heal, I hope you will benefit and grow by finding your own pathway that leads to your own healing.

In this book you will find a process to guide you and help you face your issues head on, empowering you to grow and to find new purpose in your life to come. We are changed by the roads we travel. My own journey has been full of deep emotion, intense introspection, incredible inspiration, meaningful learning, times of movement and unbelievable transformation. Each emotion helped move me, step by step, along the path I chose to take. The journey took time, effort and patience—patience not only with the process, but also with my own self.

This book is about forgiveness, a forgiveness I didn't think was possible. I write this book as one transformed by forgiveness. As I share my experiences, my questions, my deep thoughts and my vulnerabilities, imagine that I am reaching out my hand, inviting you to walk with me down a mysterious road—a road that prior to the tragedy I had never before traveled. I invite you to experience what I experienced. I will pull back the curtain so you can see the nakedness of my pain—the confusion, the reality and the miracle that occurred during this unimaginable experience. I will let you glimpse how God used the aftermath of a human atrocity to transform my undeserving heart, setting me in a direction I would never have chosen on my own.

I can assure you that in this book you will also find ways of dealing with your own painful situation. You may even become a stronger person for it. You will realize you can make it through the tough experiences of life, and that God is there to help you every step of the way.

Who am I? I am an enthusiastic woman who loves life even though life has brought many snags and challenges along the way. I have a nursing background and currently serve as Vice President of the world-renowned Gimbel Eye Centre in Calgary, Alberta, Canada. My years of executive experience in health care across Canada have been exciting, challenging and rewarding. I am a wife, and mother of two beautiful daughters; I have a wonderful son-in-law and three terrific grandchildren. I am an inspirational and motivational speaker who enjoys encouraging people to rise above the obstacles looming in their way. Most of all, I am an ordinary woman with an extraordinary experience to share.

People who have been hurt share something in common. We share the experience of being wounded. Our wounds cause us to ache, and they create a longing for the pain to subside.

But how do we heal our wounds?

In a word—forgiveness. Forgiveness is paramount; not only in healing the wounds we suffer, but also in healing the wounds we create. Healing from an emotional injury doesn't happen in a moment. It takes time, patience and a healing environment that cleanses and nourishes the wounded spirit.

This book is about forgiveness and my quest for healing. As we journey together through this book, I will try to unravel much of the mystery surrounding forgiveness. As you begin the journey toward your own healing, I invite you to feel with me the grief I experienced in the aftermath of a terrible tragedy. I invite you to open your mind, your heart and your life to the healing that can bring wonderful peace when you allow yourself to fully reflect—to see, touch, taste and feel your own experience, and to release the stranglehold grief, anger and even fear may have on your heart.

BACKDROP

DURING THE PROCESS OF WRITING THIS BOOK I realized I needed professional advice to help me create a backdrop regarding the need for forgiveness. I wanted the book to be grounded from a professional perspective, giving structure and a conceptual framework to the personal process I had encountered on my journey toward healing.

Dr. Marilyn K. Smelski, a long-time friend and fellow lady motorcyclist who has extensive background in clinical private practice graciously agreed to help. She provides individual psychotherapy and treatment for those experiencing post-traumatic stress disorder.

"People hurt one another knowingly and unknowingly; intentionally and unintentionally," I said as a prelude to our conversation. "Can you help me understand what happens to individuals when they get hurt? As a therapist, how do you help people deal with their hurts?"

We talked for almost two hours while I listened attentively, absorbing her perspectives as she described a healing process shared years ago by a mentor, a healing process that she continues to utilize in her private practice. "People have hurt each other from the beginning of time," Dr. Smelski began. "Wounded people must recognize and accept their wounds, then go through a healing process, or the effect of that hurt will prevent them from leading a full, meaningful and satisfying life. Both the attacked and the attackers need healing."

She went on to explain that wounds occur as a result of some type of trauma. This can be a big-T trauma that happened in a horrendous event, or it can be a little-t trauma, small and seemingly insignificant. Both types of trauma need healing. When a wound occurs, whether big or small, the injured person experiences either intense emotions or a feeling of numbness.

Numbed individuals are unable to identify what they are feeling. Everyone is created with feelings and emotions that are usually affirmed and confirmed in childhood. However, for whatever reason, some individuals have not had their feelings and emotions affirmed in childhood. Consequently, they aren't sure what their feelings are. It doesn't mean they don't have feelings; it's just that they don't recognize them or understand them.

Numbness following a hurtful situation may be short-lived, or it may go on for years. In a traumatic event, individuals can actually disconnect from their emotions as a self-protection mechanism. This disconnect helps keep them from being overwhelmed by the intensity of their feelings.

On the other hand, if the emotionally charged individual is indeed feeling something, the two most common emotions they experience when they've been hurt are anger and fear. It is normal to feel fear and anger, and both of those emotions can be present at the same time. The important thing to remember is that we have choices in how we respond to those feelings.

When we are fearful, we are in a vulnerable state. Feelings of anxiety, apprehension and alarm invade our thoughts. We may experience the fear of being hurt all over again. Even in situations that aren't life-threatening, we may fear being unable to cope or, respond. People who are stuck in fear may be terrified of trying to do anything to change the situation. They may be afraid of their own reactions or inabilities, or of the power of the person who hurt them. They may be afraid of the actions or abilities of others.

People who are in a state of fear ordinarily respond with fight or flight, or in some situations they may even freeze. Those who freeze up sense a type of paralysis in relation to the situation. Depending on the circumstances, the fearful individual can remain frozen and incapable of action for years.

On the other hand, individuals experiencing anger do not seem as vulnerable because they give the appearance of being in control. Wounded individuals may be angry at what happened; angry with the person who caused the wound, or angry at the results of what happened. Individuals can easily get stuck in a place of anger or in a place of fear or, depending on the circumstances; they may switch back and forth between anger and fear.

When people get stuck in anger, they circle round and round it. Over time the anger deepens, causing bitterness, vindictiveness, criticism, back-biting and the need for revenge. Bitterness is an especially strong tendency in those who are stuck in anger.

People frequently deny they are wounded. Even the admission of woundedness causes fear. These people may be unwilling to go the distance to find healing for the hurt they experienced. They may even deny that healing is needed.

Whatever state wounded people find themselves in, self-protection keeps them in a cycle of woundedness. Remaining in the cycle of woundedness is like being trapped. Unresolved hurts leave individuals vulnerable, not only to their own wounds but also to sickness and disease. Scientific evidence suggests that hate actually leads to heart disease. The awareness of body sensations and the ability to release these sensations is important in the healing process.

Remaining stuck in fear and anger can eventually lead to depression, which is anger at one's self.

In depression life becomes purposeless. The loss of one's self results in difficulty interacting with others in a healthy way. Dr. Smelski commented powerfully about the need to help people find a way to heal. "The bravest people in the world face their wounds. They understand that to heal they need help. They may need help in accepting their wounds, in accepting their self-worth, or in finding a way to recommit themselves to their own future happiness and fulfillment."

I listened, fascinated, as Dr. Smelski explained that healing is holistic in nature. It involves the body, the mind and the spirit. Hope is essential in the healing process. One way of bringing hope to the hurting person is to bring God into the picture as a partner. Bringing prayer into the healing process, she said, may make the process easier.

Our personal choices are crucial in the healing process. It isn't wrong to experience anger or fear. It is important, however, to identify the feeling and to find a way to deal with it—to make the choice to move on. If we get stuck in anger, going round and round, we still have a choice to get unstuck and to move on. The same is true with fear. It is important to remember we always have choice.

Losses are the underlying reason for anger and fear. The list of losses we experience in a lifetime is limitless. A few examples might be loss of childhood, loss of health, loss of body image, finances, reputation, relationships, marriage, loss of a job, loss of a loved one, etc. To continue the process of healing, it is essential to identify those losses. After identifying the losses, it is crucial to grieve them. Grieving consists of a separate process that can overlay or be integral to the healing process. Common steps in the grieving process include denial, anger, bargaining, depression, acceptance and hope. Individuals move around and through these steps in differing patterns and at different rates.

Healing cannot just be theoretical rhetoric. Healing has to be an experience if it is to be effective. Some may think they don't deserve to heal—they can't even imagine healing the things that have hurt them. Grieving losses may cause anger to surface, fears to rise and tears to flow, but these are essential components if healing is to be successful. Grieving one's losses cannot be skipped.

Some may be afraid of grieving because intense feelings and emotions may resurface. Others may be afraid to grieve because they associate shame with the past trauma or shame in expressing their emotions. In overcoming the fear of grieving, or in dealing with any of the steps in the healing process, it helps to remember that the journey is traveled one step at a time.

After one grieves the losses, a sense of compassion for the one who caused the hurt may begin to develop. Even a small amount of compassion for that person is beneficial. While compassion does not justify their actions, it can be very helpful when you begin to understand that the hurtful one may be stuck in their own stories, or their own woundedness, unable to move on. Once the essence of compassion penetrates the depths of your soul, it becomes like a revelation. You may also develop a sense of compassion for yourself. Compassion for yourself is perhaps the biggest hurdle. Hurting people need to be compassionate and gentle with themselves in their injured places.

When a sense of compassion becomes apparent, individuals are more capable of letting go of the hurt, anger, bitterness and hatred, enabling them to move on to forgiveness.

When people find a way to forgive, they become more open to receiving joy, love and satisfaction in their life. It doesn't guarantee they will receive these gifts, but being open to receiving them is a significant breakthrough.

The final step in the healing process involves moving on to a place of serving others in spite of the wound, and even as a result of it. In my own case, Dr. Smelski indicated, writing this book is yet another step in my healing, turning my experience and learning into an opportunity to serve others.

By the end of my time with her, I knew that our meeting was meant to be. It was amazing to see how closely the theory in her healing process paralleled my own personal experience. How could she have known so intimately the details of my journey? It was very affirming to learn that the theory she described was so analogous to my very own experience.

As I listened to Dr. Smelski, the process she described literally came alive for me. I am so grateful for the perspectives she shared. They ground the things I will share with you in the pages that follow. As we talked, her comments inspired the development of a flow chart. With her input, I have designed a graphic illustration of the healing process that serves, as a model. You'll see that chart on the accompanying page. Together, Dr. Smelski and I hope that you will be able to use this process to identify your own movement and progress as you travel your own brave journey of healing.

. . . .

The Healing Process
For Emotional Wounds ™

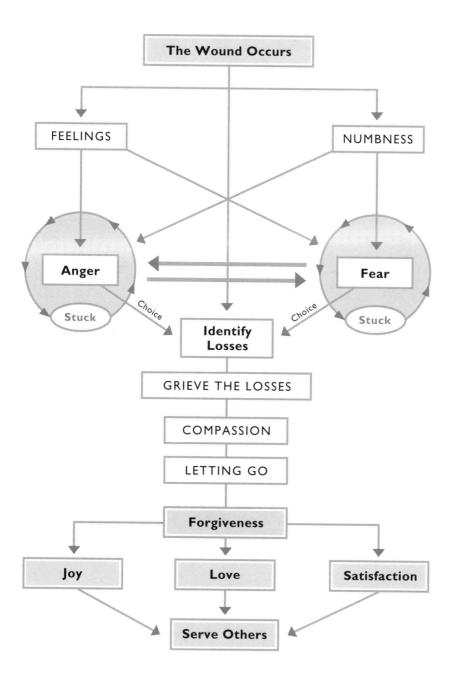

MAKING THIS BOOK PERSONAL

AT THE END OF EACH CHAPTER you will find a section entitled Personal Application intended to provide you with insights that might be applicable in your own situation.

Next you will find a section called Exploration. These questions will assist you in reflecting on your own experience. This exploration is for your eyes only, unless you choose to share your thoughts with others. As you ponder these questions you may consider using a special notebook or journal to record your thoughts or observations. Each chapter ends with a small prayer that can help bring hope and an unseen partner into the healing process.

A manual will be developed as a companion to this book. The manual will provide additional aid in applying the principles of the healing process. Workshops and seminars now in development will further aid groups in finding a way to heal the hurtful situations in their lives. Finally, inspirational keynote speeches that have the power to change the hearts and lives of audience members can be arranged. Contact information for this material may be found at the back of the book.

· ·

CHAPTER: I

MURDER:
This can't be happening

HOPE is the anchor of the soul,
the stimulus to action, the momentum
to achieve great things.

—Author Unknown

．．

I THOUGHT MY HEART WOULD STOP when I realized what my brother Rick had just said. "Soren has been murdered!"

After a deafening silence on the phone, every muscle in my body tightened into a convulsive spasm of gut-wrenching pain. I couldn't speak or breathe. Collapsing on the bed, I screamed, "No! No! No!"

My husband, Clay, heard my screams and came running. Overcome with grief, I repeated what I had just heard. "Soren has been murdered! Someone found him dead in his truck in Virginia."

Rick could hardly speak as he shared the fragmented details of our brother Soren's death. He tried to create a picture of what had happened, piecing together the skimpy information that had suddenly catapulted our life into a deep pit of disbelief, pain, chaos and questions. There were a few measly facts about when, where and how he was found, but there were no answers about who had done it, or why.

Soren was a long-distance trucker from Idaho. He had been found dead in the early morning hours outside a produce plant in Richmond, Virginia. Someone had shot him and left his body in a pool of blood, wedged between the seats and the sleeper of his beautiful big rig.

Oh, the pain! I screamed, shouted and moaned. Guttural sounds of anguish, grief and despair emanating from deep inside me echoed throughout the house. Every fiber of my body reacted to Rick's unbelievable message: murder!

I longed to crawl inside someone else's skin. I wanted to escape the excruciating realization that someone had intentionally taken my brother's life. If you could have peeled back the outer layer of my soul to peer inside, I'm sure you would have witnessed my pulsating disbelief; the horror and rage hemorrhaging deep inside my broken heart.

Clay and our youngest daughter, Shelann, encircled me with arms of love, support and comfort, trying desperately to cushion my wound. I could sense their paralysis and confusion—how could anyone help ease my pain? Yet they stayed near, allowing my agony to pour out in deep sobs of uncontrolled grief.

I felt so fortunate to have family with me when I heard the shocking news. Unfortunately our oldest daughter, Mona, was alone when she learned of the death of an uncle she adored.

That something so wretched as murder could enter the hallowed halls of my respectable family was more than my mind could grasp. The thought of someone intentionally taking the life of the brother I loved so much was beyond comprehension. My brain went into fast forward. We had suddenly been plunged into the middle of an unbelievable murder mystery and all I had to sustain me was a rapid-fire series of questions. Could this be suicide? Had Soren been depressed? Had he angered another trucker and been struck down in a fit of road rage? Did he have a gun in the truck to defend himself? Was there evidence of a struggle? Could it possibly be someone he'd offended at the produce plant?

Questions, questions and more questions, but no answers. Exhausted and bewildered, I began groping for comfort and security, for release from the horrible picture of the terror my brother must have experienced in the last moments of his life. With my mind in overdrive, I began compiling lists of things to do, arrangements needing my attention, calls to make and items to pack for the trip to Idaho for Soren's funeral.

Shelann thoughtfully found some family photo albums that brought back memories of Soren. Tall, handsome and confident, he was a true cowboy complete with trademark jeans and hat. His big smile was as memorable as his big laugh and his love for life. A big man, he lived life in a big way.

I hadn't seen him for nine months, but seeing pictures of his handsome, smiling face immediately brought back the sound of his contagious laughter and mental images of his jesting and teasing as he lovingly tormented family and friends.

We were a boisterous bunch of kids with energy to burn. We always had a lot of fun together. Riding horses as we worked the cattle on our ranch, Soren loved to pretend he was a brave Indian warrior and I loved pretending to be an Indian princess, riding swiftly and elegantly without a saddle and sometimes even without a bridle—just a piece of baler twine letting my horse know where I wanted to go.

The pictures of our childhood together reminded me of how close I was to my three brothers. I was the oldest, and the only girl. Soren was five years younger than me, while Chris and Rick were ten and eleven years younger. At a very young age, I had taken on what seemed like a surrogate mother role for my brothers.

My mother wasn't well before and after the birth of my two younger brothers, and she often visited the family doctor to get some help with what I later came to know as post-partum depression. In addition, an enormous tragedy struck my mother's family when her brother, Buster, and his two beautiful little girls were killed in a head-on collision just four miles from our home.

Mom heard about the accident just minutes after it happened. She and Daddy rushed to the scene, arriving even before the ambulance, and she held her brother in her arms as he took his last breath. Desperately reaching into the mangled back seat, my dad found the lifeless bodies of Uncle Buster's two little girls.

Mom was never the same after that. Frequently incapable of coping with the day-to-day responsibilities of being a wife and mother, she would lie on her bed staring off in the distance, unaware of things around her. I would often hear her sobs and try to comfort her, but nothing would help.

I was sad about what had happened, but my young heart and mind didn't understand the significance of that tragic accident. Too young to truly understand the depth of my mother's grief, I couldn't even begin to imagine her pain and anguish. All I wanted to do was help her.

I vacuumed, cooked, made the beds and looked after my brothers, trying to make her life easier. Dressing them, feeding them, playing with them and loving them, I cared for my brothers as best I could. I made sure they did their chores. I helped them with their homework and disciplined them while my mother nursed her wounded heart and tired body.

I even did the grocery shopping many times as Mom sat in the car, unable to greet our small-town neighbors. Perhaps she was simply unable to face the pain of talking with people about her brother's death. Unable to discuss sensitive matters of the heart or any kind of relationship issues, in those types of situations my mother would freeze up, blurt out some harsh comment, and leave the room in anger.

While it seemed that the responsibilities of mothering my three brothers fell squarely on my shoulders, I don't remember being resentful because I was happy to help. I do remember being puzzled about all the work I had to do, and I know my grandparents, aunts and uncles also sensed the heavy burden I was carrying from the comments they sometimes made.

After the months turned into years of caring for their needs, my heart attachment with Soren, Chris and Rick became much deeper than that of most brothers and sisters. I loved them with a love I'll never fully understand. That deep attachment to my brothers continues to this day, despite the geographical distance separating us. To me, the pain of losing Soren was much like that of losing a child.

Now, in recounting my own grief and exploring the reasons why I have such a close bond with my brothers, I find that I have reopened the pages of the past. Finally, after all these years, I have begun to understand the deep sorrow my mother must have been experiencing.

After looking at some of the pictures Shelann found and resting in a lounge chair to calm my nerves, I mustered the courage to call my friend Deanna who lived nearby. She literally came running. Deanna held my trembling body in her arms and rocked me as I wept uncontrollably. When there were no words to relieve my sorrow, her heartfelt compassion soothed my mangled emotions and eased the pain pressing on my wounded heart. How comforting it was to have another person sharing my sorrow. Her magic was not in her words but in what she did—she came, she cared, she held me close and she listened.

As she left, her words startled me. "Annette, you'll make it through this."

Those words shocked me in my grief, but they also brought a tiny ray of hope. Samuel Johnson said, "Hope is necessary in every condition." How I needed some hope at that moment. I almost couldn't endure the sudden onslaught of sorrow. Deanna had never experienced what I was going through, but she nonetheless recognized that I was in a terrible storm—and she believed I could make it through.

That small ray of hope was like a rainbow shining through the cloud of a dark, raging storm. The power of hope is truly amazing. A glimmer of hope can be like a tiny spark that eventually leads to a powerful flame—a flame that lights your way through the darkness.

Only a few moments after Deanna left, another special friend called. On learning what had happened, Yvonne immediately began to pray for me, right there on the phone. I remember how she pleaded with God to "wrap my grieving heart in his loving and compassionate arms of comfort."

As she prayed I felt a sense of calm come over me. As I began to relax, I realized that I was alive and that I would survive. God would get me through the next few hours, the next few days, and even the long, unbelievably painful weeks to come.

· ·

PERSONAL APPLICATION

YOU, TOO, MAY HAVE STRUGGLED with terrible news, a terrifying event or a traumatizing experience. Perhaps that experience has injured you, or wounded someone you love. While your story may not be the same as mine, it is equally important. Perhaps it has had an equally deep impact on you physically, emotionally, spiritually or financially.

Sometimes it is hard to relive or even to recall painful situations. We want to put them out of our minds because the memory brings back the anguish. But if we want to get over the hurt, we must confront the feelings.

Even though tears may come and emotions may erupt, it is good to give voice to your pain, to give a name to the feelings, the hurts and the experiences. It may feel like walking into a dark room you don't want to enter, but when you enter a dark room and lift the blinds or light even a tiny candle you can see more clearly. A dark room isn't nearly as fearful when a bit of light appears.

Facing the feelings and emotions honestly as you relive the memories is like lifting the blinds to let light into a dark room. Give yourself permission to remember and experience all the emotions you experienced with that painful event. In doing so you are taking an important step in the journey toward healing.

Spend a few moments recalling your painful situation, reflecting on the picture that comes to mind. Putting your thoughts on paper usually helps crystallize what you are thinking. You may want to record your observations in a notebook as you answer the following questions as thoroughly as possible, as well as other questions you will encounter at the end of each chapter. These questions will help you explore the implications of your feelings. Use them to help you learn to deal with your feelings in healthy, meaningful ways.

EXPLORATION

1. What painful experience have you had?

2. When did it happen?

3. What did the experience feel like?

4. How did you react?

5. Who was with you at the time?

6. What did you do or not do?

7. What were you unable to do?

8. Did anyone come to be with you?

9. How did that person's actions help you or not help you?

PRAYER

O God:

I am grateful to know that hope can be found in painful experiences. It isn't easy to walk back into the darkness of a hurtful time. I sometimes feel afraid and ashamed of my fears, tears, anger, grief and pain. Sometimes I blame myself for what happened. I need your strength to help me face those images, memories, feelings and situations that I replay over and over in my mind, decreasing my confidence and joy. Please help me process the painful experiences and find comfort and hope as I look back at the times when I have been hurt.

Amen.

CHAPTER: II

ANGER:
Dealing with pent-up emotion

ANGER is too powerful to be
overlooked and too dangerous to be ignored.
It can take us to a place of desolation.

—David Augsburger

••

WE LEFT CALGARY early the next morning. During the long, slow trip to Idaho I sat mindlessly searching the big highway trucks, scanning the face of each driver, subconsciously hoping to see my brother at the wheel. Denial of his death had set in. Searching for him relentlessly, my mind playing tricks on me, I thought that if I could just find him in one of the trucks we passed, this terrible nightmare would be over.

I was also anxious to see my other brothers, Chris and Rick. We needed to be together, to hold each other close and to share the anguish of our deep loss. I wanted to see Starli, Soren's wife of eight years, along with Pete and Niki, Soren's grown and married children from a previous marriage, as well as their children.

Clay was deep in thought as he drove. Each time we needed gas or food I insisted that we pull into a truck stop where, unbeknown to my husband, I continued my fruitless search. Soren was known as Maverick on his CB radio, but nobody I asked knew anything about a trucker named Maverick. Sitting in trucker restaurants, gazing at trucker faces and listening to trucker conversations, I dreamed of finding Soren in a booth enjoying his meal. I imagined the overwhelming joy I would experience if only I could once again feel his warm hug and hear his wonderful laughter. "This can't be true," I cried inside. "God, please help me find him."

The silence was deafening. Driving the long road from Alberta to Idaho, my heart sore with sorrow, I couldn't speak of the horrific pictures playing and replaying across the screen of my mind. Visions of terror, shouts for help and flashing gunfire jolted me awake. Every cell in my exhausted body felt the fear Soren must have experienced in his last moments of life.

I began reliving our childhood together on the farm and ranch. Recalling meaningful memories and family stories about events full of joy, about the hilarious antics of four high-spirited and fun-loving siblings, my tears turned to laughter. Our family has deep bonds of love that can never be broken, although the years and miles—and now Soren's death—have separated us. We love to tell and retell stories about things we did; memorable times that bonded us into such a special foursome.

As the oldest, I always tried to keep the boys entertained, to keep them out of trouble. Many times I resorted to dramatic play-acting as if I were sick, falling on the floor moaning and groaning, feigning a look of death. Knowing it was just a game, all three of the boys would pounce on me and begin tickling, prying open my eyes and bugging me until I jumped to my feet screaming. Then they'd chase me around the house. When boyfriends started emerging on the scene, I'd take my much younger brothers to the kitchen window and tell them to look up at the full moon, to closely examine it because it was made of cheese. I would tell them that when my boyfriend arrived we were going to climb up to the moon on a ladder and bring them back some cheese.

That crazy fairy tale lives on even today in our family get-togethers. We had such a close relationship, and my brothers trusted me so much, that I could tell them anything and they'd believe it.

It was common for Mom to be late getting ready for church. In an attempt to keep us clean and presentable, Daddy would march us around the house. We marched through the bedrooms, marched over the beds, marched on top of the dining room furniture and even marched over the kitchen table. With each step we cracked up with laughter. I can still remember the crumpled, messy beds, but more importantly I remember the fun we had just being silly together.

Driving through Montana, my mind zigzagging from happy memories to current reality, Clay and I tried to imagine what had gone so terribly wrong for Soren. Of course, no amount of speculation could possibly create the real picture for us. Sometimes the tears flowed, sometimes I was pensive, and sometimes there was an unbelieving, shivering silence. But deep inside, I was seething with anger.

Clay chose soft, relaxing music to help sooth my jangled nerves, strung as tight as the strings on a violin. When the song *God is Watching From a Distance* began to play, my violin strings broke. My pent-up emotions erupted like a volcano, and the anger boiling within me exploded into rage.

"God, how could you just watch from a distance and allow my brother to be murdered?" I screamed, shocking even myself. I began beating my fists on the window, on the dashboard, on my own legs. In my entire life I had never experienced such anger. At that moment, the focus of my anger was on God. Of course

I was angry with my brother's murderer, but with no idea who that was, the focal point of my anger became God—the God I knew, the God I loved and the God I trusted. But now it seemed like that same God had let me down. He was apparently just watching from a distance—or so the song said.

As a former pastor, Clay didn't ridicule me for lashing out at God. He didn't put me down for my shocking outburst. Instead, he spoke kindly and softly. "Annette, God understands how wounded you are. He understands your grieving heart. God understands your pain, for he too lost his only son, Jesus, to the hands of murderers who beat him and nailed him to the cross. He understands your anger and he will continue to be with you and love you even in your time of anger and despair. He also loved your brother Soren very much. Honey, just tell him how you are feeling."

Clay then gently reminded me of the Biblical text, *"When my people are crushed, I am crushed; I mourn and horror grips me." (Jeremiah 8:21-22).*

With Clay's words of comfort, I melted. Between sobs and a torrent of tears, with a contrite heart I asked how I could blame this on a God who had cradled me in his arms ten years ago during my time of brokenness and pain after a head-on highway collision. I knew it was because of his love and power that my body had miraculously recovered from that near-death experience, and that my heart had been rescued during that time of healing. How could I scream and shout at a God who had forgiven me for a horrible transgression in my own marriage?

I felt ashamed of my angry outburst at God. I felt deep sorrow that I had hurt a wonderful friend. At the same time I understood, as Nancy a friend and fellow writer once said, "God has broad shoulders. He can take my anger aimed at him when I don't know where to properly direct it. This way my anger can be unleashed. I can then come to that place in which I understand where my anger comes from, where it rightly belongs, and how I can work with it."

Just as soap and water removes most stains, tears helped soothe the sharp edges of my pain. But the most powerful stain remover was prayer. Right there in the car I poured out my heart, pleading silently for God's forgiveness. Exhausted, I fell into a deep sleep.

When I awoke, my anger at God was gone. I was ready to begin preparing for the days ahead.

. . . .

PERSONAL APPLICATION

YOU MAY BE HARBORING ANGER in your life. Anger can cause a chasm of strained or fractured relations between you and other individuals. If the anger remains unaddressed, that chasm can deepen. The inability to restore a relationship can actually result in anger turned inward, which is an unhealthy way of dealing with the problem.

By itself, however, anger is not necessarily a bad thing. On a broad continuum of emotional expression, anger can be either healthy or destructive.

At its worst, anger can cause flashes of temper or it can lay hidden and seething below the surface until something triggers an explosive reaction. Anger can be depressive, creating deep feelings of despair. Anger can be black with wrath, letting nothing in but the need to destroy its cause. Anger can be hateful, frozen and cold, or it can boil into a red face and increased blood pressure. It can explode into physical violence, abuse, assault and even murder.

Destructive anger causes many human tragedies. If anger is released without restraint, it can harm both the one holding the emotion and the one who is the target. In these situations, anger can lead to uncontrolled rage ending in destruction and death.

Anger can also be beneficial, if it motivates us to take positive action. Mothers Against Drunk Driving (MADD) was started by a group of angry mothers who had lost children as a result of drunk drivers. Their anger motivated them to start a campaign to eliminate drunk driving. That campaign resulted in a forty percent decline in alcohol-related deaths. Truthfully speaking, however, most people would rather lie than admit they are angry.

But if you do not deal with the anger you hold toward another individual, you can remain stuck in that angry place forever, unable to move forward or to heal your wound.

To heal, your anger needs to be acknowledged. If you stuff your emotions, they go undercover. One day, however, they will escape through avenues you don't expect or even understand. When that happens, you are left feeling powerless and confused. In the wake of your anger, you may needlessly hurt others.

It is important to recognize and to own up to your anger. You may need help in identifying and addressing the anger you store deep inside. Acknowledging your anger is the first step toward gaining the strength to overcome it. If you're like most of us, you were told at a young age that you shouldn't be angry. You learned that anger was wrong, that you should ignore it and put it away where no one could see it. But be sure of this: the thing you hide will someday come back to haunt you.

A positive way of dealing with anger is to talk about it. Try to understand its underlying causes. Reflect on the ways in which anger has had an impact on your life. Again, you might find it beneficial to write or talk about your anger.

EXPLORATION

1. What feelings of anger or resentment are you harboring toward another individual?

2. Where or when does anger seem to emerge in your life?

3. How is that resentment or anger reflected:
   - In your everyday life?
   - In your relationships with others?

4. How does anger influence:
   - Your self-confidence?
   - Your ability to handle stressful situations?

5. How or when does your anger affect you the most?

6. How does your anger or resentment affect the person you are angry with?

7. What can you do about your anger?

   Is there a possibility that you could benefit by some assistance with anger management?

PRAYER

O God:

Things have happened in my life that are hurtful, demoralizing or disappointing and it is hard to get over what has happened. I acknowledge and confess that I have feelings of anger and resentment toward (name the person). Please help me understand how my anger and resentment is affecting me and others near me. I realize that anger has a strong hold on me. I am having difficulty in letting go of those feelings, and yet I don't want to remain stuck in this place of anger. Help me face those things that are holding me back from a full, rich and complete life. Thank you for listening to me and for understanding how I feel.

Amen.

CHAPTER: III

CHOICES:
A cross-road of decision

CHOOSE whether a single event will be your absolute undoing or something you deal with in a positive way.

—Dr. Phil McGraw

....

AFTER A LONG DAY OF DRIVING we finally arrived at Soren's home in Aberdeen, Idaho. The house in which my mother was born and raised, had also become our family farm after Uncle Buster's death. Soren and his previous wife, Jeanette, had raised their children, Pete and Niki, in this house after Dad passed away. The house and farm held a great deal of family and community history—if walls could speak, generations of stories would be told and many secrets revealed.

The yard was crowded with cars; the house packed with people. It seemed like everyone in the small community had come to offer love, support and sympathy. They all wanted to ease the burden of pain and loss in our well-known, well-respected family.

I had to push through the crowd to find Chris and Rick. As our eyes met, we rushed together. Holding each other close, allowing the tears to flow, we refused to let go, afraid of losing more of our precious family—a family that was now broken and shattered.

Starli sobbed as I held her. Pete displayed an aura of control, but underneath the surface I could sense his emotions boiling. In losing his dad he had lost a mentor, a man who was helping him through his own marital and parenting struggles. Niki had lost her most valued cheerleader, and the grandfather who adored her children.

I hadn't seen many of the visitors for years, but they all recognized me instantly. It is always so amazing to see how our lives reconnect, even after years of absence. Everyone wanted to share what they'd come to give—love. In times of deep tragedy and severe pain the sense of community rises up, especially in small towns, and people take action. Soren had been active in the community, and now the community was actively reaching out to our family. They, too, felt our deep loss.

Our father died at age fifty-two of a massive heart attack. After his death, Chris took over the ranch, which was four miles away, and Soren took over the family farm. Soren also managed Dad's insurance business for a number of years. Soren became well-known as he traveled around the countryside meeting people and helping them with their insurance needs. He possessed the strong Cornforth genetic makeup of an outgoing personality and a fearlessness that opened doors some would have been afraid to enter. In his spare time he was a rodeo announcer. With his quick wit, his deep and expressive voice, and his abilities at public speaking he would have been a wonderful announcer. He had a captivating presence that made everyone take notice when he entered a room. His hearty laugh was memorable. Many people have commented over the years that laughter was his trademark.

When the insurance business was no longer viable, Soren tried other means of making a living. He was good at sales but needed a consistent source of income to support his family so he tried long-distance trucking. Although he enjoyed trucking, he didn't like being away from Starli. In fact, his death occurred tragically just one month before he planned to stop trucking.

We were all concerned for our frail, aging mother who was residing in a senior citizens lodge. How would she handle this tragedy? Could she cope with the news? More important, would she revert to the old patterns of mental dysfunction that had plagued her for years following the unexpected death of our father?

I will never forget the determined look in my mother's eyes, and the strength in her voice, when she spoke to me shortly after my father passed away. With clenched teeth and fists she said, "I will never get over the death of your father."

In looking back at that statement, and the way she declared herself, it seems to me now that she was pounding firm pegs of resolve in the ground—resolve to never recover. It was as if she had unwittingly made a choice of intention to remain stuck.

I now know that our lives are determined by the choices we make. Unfortunately, the determined choice my mother made that day set in motion a life of grief, bitterness, anger, depression and dysfunction that lasted more than twelve years. No amount of love, hospitalization, therapy, spiritual intervention or special care could release the chains that she unwittingly bound around herself the day she made her choice. It was a heartbreaking experience to see a once-vibrant, active and fun-loving woman reduced to a shell that no one could penetrate.

In looking back at her post-partum depression; her difficulty recovering from the death of her brother and his daughters; the death of her mother and then the death of our father; it was clearly a repeating pattern of behavior. I am not aware if grief recovery programs existed back then, but if they did she would surely have been a prime candidate. Prior to Daddy's death Mom was a vibrant, beautiful woman, always well-dressed with carefully coiffed hair and well-manicured nails. Stylish and happy, she was a high-spirited mate for my father. Daddy was always proud to have Mom by his side. Her life revolved around my father, who was the epitome of community service and leadership. He helped found the Soil Conservation District that stands as a monument to his leadership. He was a leader in the Miss Aberdeen Pageant, and his organizational abilities complemented other members of the organizing team. His public persona was dignified and effective. He was even honored posthumously for his efforts in ensuring ambulance services were available in Aberdeen.

A compassionate man, he was quick to respond to families who were hurting. Mom would bake pies and cakes for those who were struggling, but it was Daddy who went to visit them. He often took me along and I watched him comforting neighbors and friends with empathy and concern.

When Daddy became interested in politics, his ability to publicly communicate his concern, logic and options for resolution on issues made him a natural candidate for political office. He served as Idaho State Representative for a number of years and dreamed of one day being the Governor.

During his time in the legislature I had the distinct privilege of being a page in the Senate. What a tremendous learning experience. Working with Senators each day, I realized that I could comfortably associate with people responsible for making and upholding the laws of the land. During my free time, I would slip into the gallery of the House of Representatives to watch my dad in action as he debated the issues before the House. I was so proud of him! Despite his humble background and his lack of post-secondary education, he was always professional, ethical and well-respected.

Through that experience as a page I learned valuable lessons that I carry with me to this day. I learned that regardless of your background or stage in life, your opinions are valuable. You should never be afraid to speak up. I learned that it is okay to disagree, and that disagreement does not mean rejection. I learned that you can still be friends with people even though you have different backgrounds, personalities and opinions.

I saw my dad model those principles so clearly. After vehemently disagreeing with another state representative as they debated a piece of legislation, my dad would approach his opponent and put his arm around his shoulder. Rising above the debate and disagreement, together they would go off for lunch.

It is unfortunate that the world doesn't seem to understand that principle. So many relationships are destroyed due to "differences." In my view, differing opinions, personalities and perspectives help us see situations more clearly than we can when we use only our own nearsighted vision.

Mom was so proud of Daddy, and she loved to accompany him in his official duties and roles. She loved the glamour and excitement that his public personality brought to her life, and together they made quite a stunning couple.

I'll never forget the deep emotion and even the disbelief my dad expressed as he reported on his visits to mental institutions across the state. His observations and his anger at what he had seen became a catalyst in drafting legislation that made historic changes in how mental health patients were treated in Idaho at that time. Little did he know that one day, after he was gone, his wife would need the services of the very institutions he had helped to improve.

Our dad also spent long hours working in the fields making a living, raising cattle and planting, irrigating and harvesting the crops. After Uncle Buster was killed he tried to help my mother's family put their shattered lives back together. Crucial decisions had to be made quickly, and Dad and Mom were away a lot helping make those decisions. I was left to care for my brothers.

When Daddy died, our mother's world collapsed. She no longer had a need to live. Her life had been focused on Daddy's world, but now that world had evaporated. Without a world of her own, she lost interest in herself and in her surroundings. She didn't cook or clean. She lost interest in her family. She lost interest in her community. She even lost interest in her appearance. She became depressed, despondent and terrified of being alone.

When my brothers went away on a two-day hunting trip she was so terrified of being alone she called Ray, a divorced neighbor, suggesting they get married. They were married by the end of the day! That marriage was a disaster. She had nothing to give to Ray. I can't imagine how trapped she must have felt, in a new relationship with a man she didn't really know and didn't love.

She didn't love him, but she didn't want to be alone. What a conundrum! After several months she asked me to come to Idaho and help her get a divorce. I booked vacation time and an appointment with a lawyer, and flew to Idaho only to learn on the way to the lawyer's office that she had changed her mind. That happened on three separate occasions. I finally set a boundary, telling her that I would not come again for that purpose. Either she would have to live with her decision to remain married to Ray, or she would have to find someone else to help her with a divorce.

She remained in the marriage for many years until Ray died of cancer, although at times being together was a terrible trial for them both. Prior to and during her marriage to Ray her behavior became bizarre and obsessive-compulsive. Her rituals and eating habits were foreign to us, and her unnatural thought patterns and emotional outbursts made her difficult to be around. If she was able to coax someone into her car, she would keep her passenger captive for hours, losing track of time driving aimlessly around the small town of Aberdeen or out into the countryside until her car was almost out of gas. Her captives, usually former friends, were terrified by her behavior and the things she discussed.

Her kitchen was full of rotten, moldy food and take-out containers full of decayed leftovers. One of my brothers arranged for Meals on Wheels, but she screamed at the folks bringing the food, refusing the help that could make her life a little easier and healthier.

It seemed I couldn't please her. Gifts were left unopened or unused, yet she wouldn't let me forget if I failed to send one. She lashed out with hurtful comments that stabbed deep into my heart. One day in frustration she screamed that she hated me because I had always been so close to my dad.

It seemed like she had no interest in my family or in our life. To the day she died she had no idea of what our life was like— of the work we did, the joys we experienced, nor the difficulties. Meaningful conversations were impossible. Even shopping expeditions to make her life or surroundings more pleasant turned into events of disappointment and public embarrassment.

It is painful to recount this picture of my mother, but it shows the depth of her grief and her woundedness, along with her inability to move on. Several times over the years we attempted to help by committing her to mental institutions or psychiatric units of general hospitals. She was terribly angry with all of us for her hospitalization, but she would never discuss it after she was released. It seemed like she was ashamed of being in a psychiatric facility, yet we as family members carried no shame in that regard. We only longed for her to be well.

We learned from her psychiatrist that she had never properly grieved the loss of Daddy. She had only made a choice not to recover, and she was stuck. In gently approaching my mother in an attempt to explore her feelings about how she felt about the death of our father, she could not enter into a discussion. She kept saying she didn't know how she felt. She would start crying or screaming, or leave the room. As I look back, I remember observing those same behaviors years earlier when her mother passed away. It was as if she had numbed herself in her place of pain. Now she could not allow even the most compassionate gesture to help her open the door to what she might be feeling. She may have been terrified of her feelings. Whatever the reason, she stood constant guard over that door, keeping the dark closet locked and barred. No one could possibly see what was inside.

The geographical distance between us left me feeling helpless and far removed in helping my mother. There was little I could do. I will forever be grateful to my brothers for the years of pain and turmoil they endured in my absence. I have also felt a deep sadness at how her life became so lonely after losing my dad. She needed people so desperately, but her behavior pushed away the very people she needed.

After my mother passed away, our daughter Shelann, a psychologist, was able to put my mother's situation into perspective. "The things your mother did may have been the only way she knew how to grieve," said Shelann. That poignant comment resonated deeply for me. The way my mother behaved may indeed have been the only way she knew how to mourn Daddy's death, and she didn't realize she had any other choice.

I must add that in spite of the tragic difficulties I personally encountered in my relationship with my mother, I realize I am a stronger woman today because of her.

As a family we were afraid that Soren's death would once again plunge our mother into deep depression. However, her aging brain didn't allow her to fully grasp the true reality of this horrendous picture, and her grieving was short-lived. She seldom spoke of Soren's death except in short, terse comments.

Of course, that may simply have been her form of self-protection, of keeping the thought of Soren's death away from the locked door inside her mind.

Ten days elapsed between Soren's death and the funeral. Complications surrounding the homicide investigation, identification and final release of his body gave us more time to be together, to talk, grieve and prepare.

We three surviving siblings were determined to participate in the service, to celebrate Soren's life. I remember telling Mom what we were planning to do.

"Why are you going to do that?" she asked.

"Because we loved Soren so much and we want to celebrate the life we had with him," I replied.

Standing together, arm in arm, before the huge crowd of people was a bonding and meaningful experience for the three of us. In our tribute we shared Soren's poetry and our thoughts, memories, laughter and love, as well as our deep sorrow. The personal choice the three of us made to publicly give voice to our pain brought strength, hope and healing. It helped us realize that we could make it through this ordeal.

As we stood at the podium together, supporting one another, I looked down at Mom in the front row watching her three children openly and publicly expressing their feelings regarding Soren's death. The expression on her face was one of disbelief.

If only Mom had been able to express herself, I thought sadly, maybe the years of loneliness and heartache would not have been so cruel for her.

One day about six weeks after Soren's funeral, thinking back to my mother's choice to not get over the death of my father, I also made a choice. I resolved not to let Soren's death destroy me. I made a conscious decision to not let the callous cruelty of another person take away my passion and zest for life.

"I want to be happy again," I said to myself. "I don't want this ugly picture to control, confine or consume me. Soren was so happy and full of life. He wouldn't want my life to end because of his death. I will forever miss him, but I believe he would want me to continue with a happy life."

Wilma Derksen, whose young daughter was tragically murdered in 1984, says that, "Death due to violence can leave such deadly wounds in the surviving family members that it can actually rob them of the ability to manage their lives." I was determined to rise above what had happened. I wanted to not only survive, but with God's help I wanted to somehow even grow from the experience. I wanted my life after Soren's death to be a positive testimony even though I had no idea what that would include.

It isn't always easy to find happiness in ourselves, and it is not possible to find it elsewhere. David Niven said, "We assume that both happy and unhappy people are born that way. But both kinds of people do things that create and reinforce their moods. Happy people let themselves be happy. Unhappy people continue doing things that upset them."

My choice to be happy helped enormously in the ensuing months. With that decision I took back control of a situation that had thrown me out of control. It didn't mean that every day would be happy, or that unhappiness would never again appear—grief comes and goes, like the ebb and flow of the tides—but as I later realized, with that choice I began my journey of healing.

Personal Application

L IFE IS ABOUT CHOICES. You make choices every day, and many times throughout each day. In the routine patterns of everyday life your decisions may seem small and insignificant, or they may seem strategic and important—suddenly, out of the blue, you can be faced with a choice that affects you forever. Personal decisions can create opportunities for affirmative growth and strengthening of character, or they can be debilitating and devastating.

Through your choices, you have the power to create the direction your life will take. *Choices: An Adventure of a Lifetime* is perhaps the most enlightening self-development seminar my husband and I have ever taken. I don't believe it was by chance that I attended that seminar just three months before Soren's death. In that memorable experience, among other very positive actions, I was able to forgive my mother for her inability to properly mother us.

In my softening heart, a sense of compassion for her wounded-ness replaced the resentment against her that I had carried inside for so long. For the first time I understood that she may have experienced events in her childhood and adult life that she had never overcome, not realizing that she even had a choice.

The freedom that comes with exerting choice, with the knowledge that your choice can make all the difference, is exciting. If you do the same things you have always done, you will get the same results. But you have a choice. Realizing that you have a choice gives you power. The most important choice you have is your choice of attitude. No one can take that choice from you. Every day you must choose how to embrace the day. You alone are in charge of your attitude. You can't control how others behave. You may not understand why they do what they do, or even who they are. Your choice of attitude, however, can help you through every experience, every day.

EXPLORATION

1. When have you been deeply wounded by someone, or suffered a major loss or disappointment?

2. What choices did you make that helped your recovery?

3. Thinking back, were there times when you were stuck?

   What choices did you make that held you there?

   What helped you get unstuck?

4. What messages are you still telling yourself and others about this circumstance?

   Are you willing or unwilling to rise above what happened?

5. Do you sometimes feel trapped in a whirlpool of negative thoughts about another person?

   Do you feel dragged down by circumstances, or negative thoughts about yourself?

   If your answer is yes, list those thoughts.

6. List some positive choices you can make that will help you overcome the obstacles you face in this circumstance.

PRAYER

O God:

I am so grateful you've created me with the ability to
make choices. Thank you for the things I'm learning about the
power of my own choices. Even though I have had some hard
and hurtful experiences to deal with, I don't want to be mired
in discouraging and depressing thoughts. I need a lifeline to hang
onto and to lift me up. I need help to find the courage, strength
and ability to choose ways of thinking past the circumstances
that seem so awful. Help me find positive ways of responding
to this situation. Thank you for helping me find ways of making
constructive choices—choices that will help me gain a strong
foothold and that will lead me out of the dark places
that cling like chains around my wounded heart.

Amen.

CHAPTER: IV

CRISIS:
Coping with everyday life

GOD grant me the serenity to accept the things I cannot change, courage to change the things I can and the wisdom to know the difference.

—Reinhold Neibuhr

· ·

MANY TRIBUTES AND MUSICAL NUMBERS dignified the last hour we spent with Soren. In honor of a fallen comrade, a cavalcade of shiny big trucks led the funeral procession through the small farming community to a well-manicured cemetery in the countryside where Soren was to be buried near our dad.

When I spied the mound of dirt beside the dark, gaping hole that would receive my brother's body, I thought my heart would break. This was it—I had to let go. I had touched Soren's cold, stiff hands and kissed his lifeless cheek. I had even laid my head on his chest, straining to hear the faintest heartbeat, hoping that somehow this horrible scene was just a cruel nightmare.

How could we leave Soren's body in this cold, dark, forsaken grave? Somehow we made it through the graveside service. Soren was a Vietnam war veteran; military traditions were part of the final goodbye. The eerie sounds of distant taps and the chilling staccato of rifle shots punctuated the crisp cold air, shocking me again into awareness that this was for real.

We left the cemetery knowing that we were closing this chapter of the story. Family and friends gathered at a local church where the community had lovingly prepared a reception. It had been ten days of emotional upheaval. We had suffered through long, sleepless nights, telling and retelling the story of Soren's death as each new family member and friend arrived. We tried desperately to bring some semblance of reason, to find answers to the questions plaguing us. Who had done this despicable thing? Was it someone he knew? Why had he been killed? What was the motive? Was there any evidence? To all these questions we had no answers.

The next day we returned to Alberta. The following day I went back to work. Flowers, cards and letters poured in. People were kind, loving and patient, but I was a mess. I felt numb after all that had been packed into the ten days of doing what grieving families do—just trying to survive the onslaught of emotions, people, plans and helping each other navigate the nightmare. For several days at work I couldn't sort through my mail, I couldn't remember important telephone numbers, and I even had difficulty remembering the password to turn on my computer. It seemed as though the trauma of my brother's murder had scrambled my mind to such an extent that I could barely cope with the mundane activities of daily living.

My mind was constantly on Soren. I would no longer hear his voice on the other end of the telephone. The silly nickname "Sisty Ugler" from Cinderella had stuck with me for years. In fun he loved to call my work in the middle of the day, shocking my assistant with the demand, "Let me talk to my ugly sister." Several times he got me out of a boring hospital board meeting with his demand, laughing like crazy when I answered. Together we would howl over his craziness.

Recalling those special memories, the echo of his laughter rang in my ear—laughter that was stopped short by the sound of gunfire.

For weeks I purposely chose to wear a scarf, pin or bracelet that in some way reminded me of Soren. Several times throughout the day I would touch the item and receive a moment of comfort as if touching a memory. One pin had special significance. Fashioned of two finely crafted entwined hearts, it symbolized a particularly meaningful card stating that even though I'd lost someone special, I still could carry him close in my heart.

At work, at home and at church I managed to wear a mask of smiles, pleasantries and humor, but my sorrow was always close at hand. It lay hidden under layers of "I'm okay" messages that I constructed to convince others that I was recovering, possibly to protect myself from the continuing pain and grief. While the visible tears began to diminish, my silent tears were never far away.

Over the months, thoughtful individuals magically placed cards, pictures, flowers, an artistic butterfly, meaningful quotes and a box of treasured angel cards in my office. In the months after Soren's death, their silent support touched me deeply. Each gesture was like a touchstone helping me know that my friends understood that healing isn't complete just because the visible tears have stopped.

We must never underestimate the value of compassion. Just knowing someone is thinking of you in your struggle helps ease the burden. I learned through their tokens of compassion that it is never too late to share your heart with a wounded person. A gentle act might be just the lift needed to help navigate a rough spot in the road.

The days and weeks went by in fast forward. I was a busy corporate executive with projects, meetings, traveling and speaking engagements, along with household and family responsibilities. But in my quiet desperation, I felt out of control. I knew I was not coping well. In executive meetings I found myself losing concentration, unable to remain focused on the issues. To re-enter the flow of conversation I'd have to shake my head, or pinch myself. My desk piled higher and higher with stuff that I needed to file or discard, but I found it hard to let go of the familiar, comfortable stuff.

At times grief flooded over me. Standing on the fourth floor of the building where I work, peering over the balcony railing at the atrium below, I saw people talking, laughing and hurrying, absorbed in their own worlds, unaware that I stood watching them with eyes brimming with tears. I had the angry urge to scream out, "Stop! Don't you know my brother has been murdered? How can you scurry about in a mindless frenzy?"

I became terrified of walking alone from my car across the a dark parking lot. I would wait in my car or at the door of a building until I could walk near someone—anyone, so if someone jumped out at me I could scream for help, knowing the person near me would hear my cry.

My quest to know who had killed Soren escalated. I was constantly puzzling over who it could have been. I imagined perfectly normal men as capable of murder. One evening I even saw the imaginary word Murderer written across the foreheads of a dozen men in a grocery store.

I told no one about these bizarre thoughts, but I began to think I was losing my mind. I knew I was experiencing a crisis in coping. When I finally shared some of my fears and fantasies with Clay, he lovingly suggested, "Honey, do you think you could benefit from some grief counseling?"

I was startled by this statement, but not offended. I had a deep trust in my husband, in his skill as a pastor along with the training he had taken as a chaplain. He must have been giving some thought to my bizarre behavior, because he had the name of a grief counselor on the tip of his tongue. I immediately placed a call to the hospital chaplain he suggested.

When I described Soren's death and some of my struggles, Chaplain Bob Glasgow agreed to see me that very day. Even though I had been denying it, I knew that my emotions were scarred and that to cope, I needed help.

When I called the grief counselor, I made a choice to act. I acted out of fear—fear that I was losing my mind, but I also made that choice out of hope—the hope that someone could help me. In describing this phenomenon, LuAnn Mitchell-Halter says, "Our choices are often based on either hope or fear. Fear can make us overly cautious and stop us from reaching our true potential in a situation. But the power of hope is truly amazing. It is hope that gives us the ability to overcome the odds, and achieve what some say… is impossible."

Bob is small in stature, but with a huge capacity to care. His warmth and his wonderful heart have brought comfort and restoration to countless individuals over the years. He welcomed me into his office and listened attentively as I tearfully poured out my story. He gave me several books to read on grief recovery, but he said there was very little literature dealing with death due to violence, or with the death of an adult sibling.

I devoured every book and article I could get my hands on, and every Thursday for weeks I visited this wise, gentle healer. Each time we met he would ask a question or make a statement that encouraged me to ponder, reflect and then express what I was feeling. Henry Nouwen said, "When we honestly ask ourselves which persons in our lives mean the most, we often find that it is those who instead of giving advice, solutions or cures, have chosen rather to share our pain and touch our wounds with gentle and tender hands. The friend who can be silent with us in a moment of despair or confusion, who can stay with us in an hour of grief and bereavement, who can tolerate not-knowing, not curing, not-healing, yet face with us the reality of our powerlessness. That is the friend who cares." That is the kind of friend I found in Bob. Having someone to listen with a gentle sense of direction was an important part of my healing.

Together we talked about what was happening to me. His wisdom and skill in bringing alternate perspectives to my sometimes distorted perceptions were so beneficial.

One statement in particular I remember clearly.

"Annette, sometimes when there has been a death due to violence, the surviving family member has a need for revenge."

He didn't say another word. He didn't make a judgment about whether revenge was good or bad, and he didn't ask any questions. He just made a simple statement. We sat in silence as I pondered the word revenge.

"I know that in the early stages after learning of Soren's violent death I was so angry that I wanted something terrible to happen to the person who took my brother's life," I said quietly. "But it is important for me to get well. I don't have energy to put toward gaining revenge for my brother's murder. Hurting someone or causing injury to the one who has taken Soren's life will never bring Soren back. Revenge will never help. Revenge will only beget revenge."

I realized I had made two powerful choices. I was choosing to get well, I was also choosing to not go down the path of revenge.

Through reflection and open discussion, during those counseling sessions I learned many things. I learned that it is important to talk about your feelings and to identify what hurts. I learned it is vital to understand how the trauma is affecting you in your life and in your relationships. I learned it is essential to talk about the anger and the fears, to explore them in the hopes of gaining understanding. By facing the emotions and naming them our understanding increases. Most importantly I learned I didn't have to remain stuck in a place of anger or fear.

I spoke openly of my fear about being alone in the dark. As we explored those feelings I realized that my panic was possibly related to the horrendous trauma Soren had experienced alone in the darkness. I also remembered that many years ago in Ethiopia, during our three years there as missionaries, I, too, had experienced extreme fear.

I remembered the absolute terror I felt crouching in the front seat of a car while being repeatedly shot at from a passing vehicle. I have never experienced such fear in my entire life. On another occasion, while walking alone on a quiet street I was violently attacked and dragged into an alleyway by a strong, athletic man. Again the terror was incredible as I fought for my life. By the grace of God, I was able to escape without physical injury. Miraculously the four rolls of toilet tissue I was carrying became heavy as bricks as I pummeled my assailant. Physically I was fine, but the psychological damage was yet to manifest itself.

Soren's violent encounter had apparently triggered memories that caused old fears to resurface. Through talking and logical reasoning, I realized that Soren's death did not place me in any greater risk of being attacked than I had been before his death. I also came to the conclusion that my fear of being alone in the darkness was irrational. What a relief it was to lay aside those unfounded fears.

After that counseling session, I never again experienced that type of fear. When we uncover uncomfortable emotions we feel vulnerable, and feeling vulnerable isn't comfortable. Flashbacks and memories can paralyze us, making it impossible to process those memories into the realities of today. Sharing our fears and feelings with someone removed from the situation can often help put things into perspective.

"Each risk we take, each time we move out of what feels comfortable, we become more powerful," says Susan Jeffers in *Feel the Fear and Do It Anyway*. Facing my fears and walking away from them was energizing and liberating, and that placed me in a powerful position to move on.

Then one evening a scene on television triggered a particularly awful flashback. A gun was suddenly pointed directly at the camera at close range, instantly filling me with a feeling that it was pointed at me. Immediately I was in the truck with Soren, physically and emotionally experiencing the terror and helplessness I imagined he must have felt as he faced the man who shot him. I screamed and ran from the room, engulfed in sobs.

Reliving that experience was shocking, but it also helped me understand what Soren must have gone through. The trauma of that experience also caused me to relive the horror of being shot at in Ethiopia some twenty years earlier. That terrible flashback was so real that I actually found myself physically crouched low as if in the car, trying to escape the bullets. My heart beating wildly, I screamed in terror and prayed for protection. When the terror subsided I was exhausted and could barely move.

Viewing Soren's body before the funeral, I needed to see and touch the wounds on his face and head. In my nursing experience, I had examined wounds hundreds of times. When I lifted the small bandage on his hand, I could see where he had desperately tried to stop the bullets. I longed to understand what had happened to Soren. I had an insatiable appetite for details. I'll never forget cornering an innocent forensic pathologist at a party. It seemed like no one was safe from my quest to know everything. I literally pummeled him with questions regarding the structures of Soren's brain that were damaged by the bullets. That discussion was so valuable—it helped me realize that Soren did not suffer long. He died almost instantly after the second shot.

During this time my brother Rick was also in search of information. One evening he was meandering on his bicycle through a truck stop in Idaho. He found a truck just like the one Soren drove. He stopped and talked with the driver. Before long, Rick had convinced the driver to help him re-enact the crime scene. He, too, needed details to help him bring clarity to the picture.

During that time I viewed my brother's murderer as a monster. Bob did not trivialize the violence, but he tried to help me see it through a different lens. Perhaps the monster perception was the reason I was seeing normal-looking men as murderers. Was my logical mind beginning to convince me that normal-looking people can also be responsible for terrible things?

Bob pointed out that a person doesn't have to appear evil to take someone's life. He also taught me that the anniversary of a loved one's death, or the anniversary of a traumatic event, can be a particularly sensitive time since the memory of the event often causes deep sadness. He reinforced two important principles I had learned at Choices—until we find a way to deal with the pain, nothing will change; and we cannot heal what we do not acknowledge. The changes in perspective Bob gave me were invaluable and enlightening in my journey of healing. I was exhausted after each session, yet I walked away with renewed energy. Most importantly, I learned that I was actually quite normal. I wasn't losing my mind!

One day Bob said to me, "Annette, you are facing your brother's death head-on. You are a healthy woman—one day you will walk away from the pain as a strong, courageous and free woman."

Greatly relieved, I felt elated. When I asked how he knew, he said it was obvious that I was exploring my feelings and reading and writing about them. He said that in processing the details, in searching for information that would help me understand what Soren had gone through, I was walking through the pain rather than hiding from it.

With those words I truly began to feel strong and confident. I knew I was going to make it. I even sensed that my capacity for joy was returning.

At Shelann's suggestion, I also volunteered to participate in a doctoral research study that focused on the loss of an adult sibling. It was gratifying to know that my personal experience might eventually contribute to the scant pool of knowledge on the subject.

• •

PERSONAL APPLICATION

YOU TOO MIGHT BE HIDING behind a façade of "I'm okay" messages. You may be giving these messages to the world around you, or you may be giving them only to yourself.

Joyce Meyer, the author of *Beauty for Ashes,* overcame years of sexual, physical and emotional abuse. I love the title of one chapter, "The Only Way Out Is Through." Meyer says, "There are certain stages we have to go through in order to mature." These stages include facing your past, addressing the pain, and seeking help in overcoming your dysfunctional behavior. To mature and grow, you must go through these stages.

Suppressed tears and anger may emerge as you begin the hard work of recovering from hurtful experiences. Identifying the hurts of the past and addressing them—along with understanding how they affect you today—is an essential part of the healing process. You must recognize that healing takes effort. You may want to consider contacting a counselor to help you process the past.

You will never be able to change the past, but you can change how you respond to it. You can change how you react to circumstances that evoke old feelings and emotions. You can change the things over which you have control. You can't turn back the clock and recover wasted years. There is no way to mop up all those silent tears of regret, shame, bitterness and hatred. But you can move forward.

It is possible to find relief, release and even meaning in your life. The choice is yours. Don't put it off. Your crisis may have occurred in the past, but the time for change and growth is now.

EXPLORATION

1. What happened to you in the past that may be affecting your attitude, your relationships and even your successes at home, at work, in your friendships and in your community?

2. What experiences do you re-live that are hurtful, painful, frightening or possibly even debilitating?

   What are the things that trigger those memories and emotions?

3. How is a past experience affecting you? Be specific.

   - How do you relate to others?
   - How do you trust (or mistrust) others?
   - Ponder your ease or difficulty in developing and maintaining meaningful relationships?

4. What do you think about when you recall the circumstances of the past?

5. What are the things you cannot change?

6. What are the things you can change?

PRAYER

O God:

I want to be whole, but the thing that happened when
(name the event) keeps me from experiencing joy. I know that
this thing clouds my perceptions and prevents me from being the
full and complete person I am meant to be. Sometimes I get stuck
—I don't even recognize my problem until someone else helps
me realize that I am in need. Help me find a better way of dealing
with the things that trouble me. If I am in need of professional help,
please lead me to the right person. Guide me as I walk the path
that leads to healing and wholeness. At times I feel afraid, so please
give me the strength and courage I need. Remind me that you are
always with me as I work through the crisis I find myself in.

Amen.

CHAPTER: V

UNANSWERED QUESTIONS:
Seeking the answers

OVERNIGHT my anger turned to acceptance, my pain turned to purpose, and even my hatred turned to hope.

—Annette Stanwick

....

I LAY ON MY PILLOW in the blackness of night. Overwhelmed with grief, I couldn't turn off my mind. Physically and emotionally exhausted, I was tormented by unanswered questions —questions that had plunged me deep into the middle of this horrific murder mystery.

The number one question was, "Who did it, and why?"

Who had killed Soren? Even when crucial questions are unresolved and when no answers are apparent, we need to make sense out of the senselessness. We need someone to take the blame. In the darkness, I tried to determine what type of person could have done this hideous thing. It was like I was conducting my own investigation. "What type of person could have broken into Soren's truck? It must have been a deliberate, determined or desperate person. What kind of person could have beaten him terribly and then shot him twice? It must have been an angry, heartless, vicious person. What type of person could have killed my brother for no apparent reason? My answer was always the same: a callous, malicious, evil person.

One by one I listed the terrible, descriptive names—Evil, Executioner, Vicious, Wicked, Vile, Monster. I went through the alphabet, methodically listing terrible words that helped release the pent-up anger coursing through my veins.

Then in the midnight silence, I heard a voice call my name.

"Annette," said the voice, "the man who murdered your brother is deeply wounded." It was as if another name had been added to my list—"Wounded".

I was shocked. Astounded by what I'd just heard, I replied in an almost haughty manner, "So?" The voice spoke again. "Annette, I love your brother's murderer. I love your brother's murderer as much as I love you, and as much as I love your brother Soren."

I knew without a shadow of a doubt that it was the voice of God. After hearing those words, I could hardly breathe. I didn't want to believe what I'd just heard. I didn't want those words piercing my wounded heart. I covered my ears with my pillow and wrestled with my thoughts—and with God—for hours, twisting and turning and pounding on my hot, tear-stained pillow.

I knew how much God loves us, in spite of what we've done, but I didn't want to acknowledge that kind of love for my brother's murderer. I pleaded, "Please don't ask me to believe this about the one who has senselessly taken my brother's life."

As the long hours passed, familiar Bible passages flooded my mind. I had read, reread, pondered and shared those Bible passages with thousands of women at Christian retreats across Canada and the United States. I had often told the women in my audiences to insert their own names into the texts they were reading to help them understand how much God loves them, and to help them see how to apply those Biblical passages in their own lives.

Following my own instructions, I began inserting the words "your brother's murderer" into the texts flooding my mind. Slowly and reluctantly I repeated the verses: *"I love your brother's murderer with an everlasting love,"* (Jeremiah 31:3). *"While your brother's murderer was dead in sin, I died for him,"* (Romans 5:8). *"For God so loved the world, he gave his only begotten son for even your brother's murderer,"* (John 3:16).

I had often used those and other familiar passages to help other individuals in times of deep need. I had shared them with people who had stumbled, fallen and made terrible mistakes. But to apply those Bible passages to my brother's murderer was a huge leap from the theory of God's love to its actual application.

That leap was far beyond where I wanted to go that night. In my heart, however, I knew it was true. God loves us in spite of who we are, in spite of what we've done. I came to the realization that those Bible passages were indeed meant for my brother's murderer, whoever he was. In the wee hours of the morning, I realized I couldn't fight the truth of God's unconditional love any longer. I accepted the fact that God loves my brother's murderer. God had won the battle. I finally fell asleep with a deep sense of peace and release from my struggling.

The next morning I was a changed woman. Those five unbelievable words I'd heard in the middle of the night had changed me. Those words spoken by God, the author of love, will forever be seared into the flesh of my heart: "I love your brother's murderer."

I shared the story of my night of wrestling with my husband, Clay. Astounded by the incredible depth of God's love, I remember saying, "The experience I had last night was so powerful that

I hope the day will come when I can see my brother's murderer face to face and tell him how much God loves him." What a transformation! Overnight I'd been changed. I'd gone from being bitter and angry to anticipating telling my brother's assailant that God loves him. There is not a question in my mind that a miracle of God had occurred in my heart that night.

Personal Application

I T MAY BE HARD TO ACCEPT that God loves the person who hurt you. It was certainly hard for me to accept. But notice that when God's Spirit spoke to me and told me that he loved my brother's murderer, he didn't say he loved what the murderer had done. No! God abhors sin. He abhors the pain people inflict on one another. It goes completely against what he tells us to do. He tells us to, "Love one another as I have loved you."

Even though God despises the terrible things people do, he nonetheless longs to bring healing. He longs to bring healing to our lives and he longs to bring healing to those who have hurt us.

God loves everyone, and he can separate the deeds from the individual. As mere human beings, we often have a hard time making that distinction. *"Man looks on the outward appearance, but God looks on the heart." (1Sam.16:7).* We need to be open to God's leadership, to his word and to his direction. He will show us and he will help us in ways we cannot even begin to imagine.

On your own, it may seem impossible to change how you feel about the person who hurt you. It takes a supernatural act of God to change your heart and your mind, but if you truly want to heal and are open to God's leading, he is willing to give you a gift that will change you from the inside out.

Change doesn't come easily. Years of tears and resentment may have seared your heart with scars. You may feel stuck in a cauldron of feelings and memories that you don't want to recall or believe. It may be painful for you to think of the perpetrator of your pain as someone God loves, but God loves that person no matter what. However, he will never love what that person has done.

Be open to change. Be open to an experience you'll never regret. When God changes your heart it is always for the better. It can be absolutely astounding what that change can do for you.

EXPLORATION

1. What are your thoughts about the person who hurt you?

2. When you think of the person who caused your pain, what images come to mind? Be specific.

3. Describe the feelings you experience when you think of that individual and what they did.

4. What thoughts or feelings does it create for you to know that God loves the person who hurt you?

5. Describe your response to the fact that God loves that individual in spite of what they've done.

PRAYER

O God:

I am so wounded I can see only my own hurts. Help me
face my pain and assist me to identify how I feel about it. I need
to understand how my pain impacts me. I know you do not love
the evil things that people do to each other, but I am beginning
to understand that you love each one of us in spite of the things
we do. I am grateful that you love me even though I am not always
loving and kind. Help me to understand the difference between
the person you love, and the behavior of that person. Please help
me see beyond my own woundedness. Open my eyes and
my heart. Help me see the one who has hurt me the way
you see them. I know your eyes are full of compassion
and love. Please help me find a way to heal
my woundedness.

Amen.

CHAPTER: VI

ANCHORS:
Gaining strength from the past

THIRSTY hearts are those whose longings have been wakened by the touch of God within them.

—A.W. Tozer

• •

TEN YEARS EARLIER I HAD been touched by God in a different, but similarly profound, manner. Shelann and I were driving home on a busy four-lane highway in Toronto when a car in the oncoming lane suddenly veered into our path. We collided head-on. "God help us!" I remember screaming through the sound of crushing metal and shattering glass, and then it was deadly quiet. In that terrifying moment of silence, I peered down at the keys swinging back and forth in the ignition.

Feeling a crunching sensation in my back, I was alerted to the possibility that I may have a fractured spine. Paralysis immediately came to my mind. I tried to move my hands and feet. To my great relief, they moved. Looking over at my beloved 14-year-old daughter, I saw her face covered in blood. She wasn't breathing. "Breathe, Shelann!" I screamed with every ounce of strength I had. I tried to shake her, but the steering wheel pinned me. "Breathe, Shelann, breathe!" I cried again. Stretching until our fingertips touched, I squeezed her hand and felt a faint pressure in return. She was alive! "Oh God, please save my daughter," I prayed. "Don't let her die!"

Sirens echoing in the distance gave me hope. Frantic voices surrounded the car. I sensed consciousness evading me. Slipping in and out of awareness, I tried desperately to stay alert by methodically assessing each part of my body, tightening and releasing the muscles. With my knowledge as a nurse, I could sense the extent of my injuries.

When the ambulance arrived, I was barely able to whisper that I had a broken hip and possibly a broken pelvis. I knew I had a compound fractured knee because I could feel the protrusion of bones through the open wound. The crunching sensation in my chest and back meant there were numerous fractured ribs and possibly a fractured spine.

I was also able to describe the haunting picture of the gaping mouth and eyes rolled back in the head of the female driver who hit us. To this day I'm amazed at my assessment skills while near death. I was even able to tell the police where to locate my husband.

What a relief when I sensed they had removed Shelann from the mangled mess and I heard the sirens fading in the distance. I wish I could have seen the face of the police officer who responded to my stupid question, motivated by pure vanity: "How does my face look?"

"Lady, you look beautiful," he responded dryly.

It took forever for the Jaws of Life to pry apart the crushed metal encasing me like a tomb. I was amazed at the relief when the steering wheel was cut away. Breathing was difficult. The gurgling deep in my chest and throat alerted me to the severe damage my lungs had sustained. I drifted in and out of consciousness to the sounds of bending metal as the hydraulic equipment strained to release me from the mangled wreckage.

Working carefully and efficiently, the paramedics strapped me into a neck brace and onto a back board. I'll always remember the urgency in the paramedic's voice calling to the ambulance driver, "Step on it, I'm losing her!" Then the sound of sirens faded into blackness.

When I came to, dozens of people in the emergency department were working to save my life, to keep my damaged lungs functioning, to replace lost blood, to stabilize my broken bones. Being an experienced nurse I recognized every action they took, and often gave them clues to what I needed. I knew the situation was serious when I heard someone say there were no more ventilators so they had to "bag" me.

I had bagged numerous patients when all the life-saving ventilators were in use on critically ill patients, but this time the bagging rhythm didn't seem to be working on me. I remember reaching out with weakened hands and taking over, performing the procedure myself to artificially keep me breathing and bring blessed relief to my wounded lungs.

When I asked about my injuries, they seemed reluctant to tell me. That made me frustrated, and my assertive self resurfaced. I let them know that I was a nurse and that I could handle the bad news. With that, they confirmed that I had a fractured hip and pelvis, a fractured knee, eleven fractured ribs, a flail chest and badly damaged lungs. They were unsure if I had a fractured spine.

The news was bad. I was in critical condition, but I had no fear. The information shared confirmed what I already knew. This reduced my anxiety and frustration. I then actually relaxed and drifted into a dreamy, medicated drowsiness.

Sometime later, when I woke, I asked about Shelann. All they would say was, "She's okay." In frustration I again mouthed the words, "I am her mother and a nurse. Please let me know." Relenting, they told me that Shelann had several broken ribs, some facial lacerations and a possible fractured tracheal ring. That explained why she had difficulty breathing at the scene of the accident. They were planning to transfer her to the Intensive Care Unit at Toronto's Sick Kids Hospital. We later learned she also had a fractured jaw.

I felt so helpless. I could do nothing for my precious daughter in her time of greatest need. All I could do was place her in God's hands. I remember reciting the 23rd Psalm. One excerpt was particularly poignant: *"Yea, though I walk through the valley of the shadow of death, I will fear no evil. Thy rod and thy staff, they comfort me."* Reciting this verse… I added an impassioned plea— *"and I know they will comfort my precious daughter."*

With that, I relinquished my hold on her. I was powerless, voiceless and incapable of doing anything to help her, or myself. Normally a woman of action and ability, I was reduced to total reliance on God.

My husband arrived with terror in his eyes. I motioned for Clay to go to the Sick Kids Hospital with Shelann. I couldn't bear the thought of her being alone during this scary, painful time. However, the staff told Clay that he should remain with me. They said that Shelann would be okay, but I was in critical condition. As they wheeled Shelann out the door, he prayed for us both.

I began experiencing discomfort in my abdomen. I sensed it swelling. I let the staff know, but they did nothing. No one seemed concerned. The tension in my abdomen continued to increase. I reached out and grabbed the supervisor, mouthing the words, "I'm bleeding internally. Do something or I'll die." I even motioned for them to measure my girth if they didn't believe me. They soon rushed me to the operating room and worked for several hours repairing my badly lacerated liver. I learned from that surgeon months later that several times during the surgery they thought they had lost me.

Once the liver was repaired, I was transferred by helicopter to the renowned Sunnybrook Trauma Centre.

I was apparently unrecognizable, with the ventilator, chest tubes, traction, catheters and IV lines along with the fact that my face, neck and shoulders were so swollen. My eyes were swollen tightly shut and I was unable to see anything—I could only respond to sounds and touch. The tube inserted in my trachea for artificial breathing prevented me from speaking. With thirteen broken bones, my body was like mush. It was too painful to move. The medication they administered induced a paralysis so my body wouldn't fight the ventilator. I lay in total darkness—unable to see, unable to speak and unable to move.

On the third day of our crisis I motioned to Clay for a paper and pencil. With the fingers of one hand I pried open my left eye, giving me a small, blurry peephole. With the other hand I feebly wrote, "I'm dying. I want you to marry again!"

Little did I know the crushing blow that had been dealt to Clay. The doctors had given him no hope for my survival. My body was so broken and traumatized they didn't really believe I could recover. Now my own words had shattered what little hope he had left. Devastated by my comments, all alone that night he prayed, wept and walked the floor, seeking peace and healing.

Unbeknown to me, family, friends and church groups across Canada and the U.S. were praying—some praying round the clock.

I was in intensive care for almost four weeks. In spite of all that was being done for me, I felt alone in my dark, almost paralyzed cocoon. Yet even though I knew I was dying, I wasn't afraid. I was totally relaxed, at peace with my impending death. I prayed that God would look after my wonderful husband and my precious daughters.

Little did I know I was living on the edge of a miracle. Despite the aloneness, I had the most incredible companion nearby. I felt secure, with an overwhelming sense of being cradled in tender, loving arms. I knew I was being cradled in the arms of God. The sensation brought an incredibly deep peace. I longed to be in that place of peace and love forever.

I heard a voice saying, "Annette, I can't take away all this pain and discomfort, but I will never leave you nor forsake you. My strength is sufficient for you. I love you with a love that is without end. I laid down my life for you and I will never let you go."

After more than three weeks of intensive care and multiple surgeries, the ventilator was removed and the medications reduced. When Clay walked in the door later that day, he knew something dramatic had happened. I was alert and able to speak—although only two or three words at a time. I had to tell him what had happened. Through breathless whispers I shared my amazing experience with him. The tears streamed down his face and mine. The verbal picture I painted for him of my experience with God was exactly what he had been praying for. There was not a doubt in either of our minds—and in the minds of the doctors and staff—that truly we had experienced a miracle.

I felt overwhelmed that God had chosen to come so close to me with his love and attention during my time of need, especially when I considered some mistakes in my life that made me feel so unworthy. Then I realized that God had forgiven me. His personal touch and healing power was a clear demonstration that his love, acceptance and forgiveness are gifts that come from his heart. Those gifts were not given because I had earned or deserved them in any way. Those gifts were pure and unconditional and they left an indelible impression on my heart.

Recovery was hard and painful, but I was so full of gratitude for God's presence that I put forth every ounce of energy I could.

Rehabilitation was intense. It seemed like I was training for the Olympics. I spent several hours each day exercising, relearning to walk and rebuilding muscles that had atrophied from long months of inactivity, having suffered the assault of so many surgeries —eight in total.

Despite limitations that at times seemed insurmountable, I realized that without the pain there would be no gain. I knew that no one could do the work for me. I had a long way to go, but the only way I could improve was to put my heart and soul into recovery. Through almost five months of hospitalization and intense rehabilitation, I learned many things about myself, about life and about God.

I learned that God is real, personal and incredibly loving. I learned that God loves me in spite of my flaws and failures, and in spite of all the times I ignored or avoided him. I learned that his strength was all I needed, and that he would never leave me. I learned that he could take the tough stuff in my life and turn it into something good, if I was open to receiving the goodness.

My courage and positive attitude became a source of encourage-ment to my therapists and to other patients who watched me working so hard and being so joyful with my tiny day-to-day improvements. As I spent time in prayer each day, giving thanks for my new strength, I began to realize that my problems weren't going away, but the way I viewed my problems was being transformed. As I praised God, I found more and more energy to pour into recovery.

During this time Shelann was also recovering beautifully, and soon she returned to school, staying with one of our friends so Clay could spend time with me at the hospital which necessitated a 45 minute drive each way everyday. Although I didn't know it at the time, the lessons I learned during my crisis and recovery would become my anchors. Those lessons were preparing me for some phenomenal opportunities to later share the truth of God's love after I had fully recovered. Still later, after my brother's death, my anchors again kept me grounded in God's love.

The entire amazing experience changed me. I had a story to tell, an experience that begged to be shared. More important, I had a message that needed to be heard about a personal God who loves us more than we can possibly imagine. My story was about a God who comes to comfort us in our crisis and who gives us the strength to rebuild our lives.

I never could have imagined how that painful experience would propel me into the speaking circuit across North America. It was as if my suffering had become a training ground, and I had become a witness to God's work in me. I had so many scars, but those scars were constant reminders of God's tender touch.

The message that I began to share was that if God could heal and transform me, he was also willing and able to heal and transform others. I longed for my audiences to understand God's ability to bring meaning to their painful experiences and circumstances when they are open to his healing power.

My message was about how God lavishes his wondrous love, acceptance and forgiveness on us. It was about his voice, his comfort and his peace—a peace that is beyond our human understanding. I was in love with Jesus Christ, and I was anxious to tell people how I had come to know him so personally.

Ten years ago I'd been awakened, rescued and restored by God's tender touch, and it had changed the direction of my life. For ten years that experience had been my anchor. After Soren's death, I again recognized the deep thirst I had first experienced ten years earlier. I was thirsty for relief. I needed to drink from the river of God's love. My soul, parched by grief and sadness, longed for God's healing touch, a touch that would somehow transform this madness into a place of wonderful peace.

In the depths of my grief over Soren's murder, I was again struggling to find my anchor. I knew that if only I could sense God's presence and power again, I would not only survive this place of pain, but with God's help something meaningful could emerge out of the senseless tragedy of my brother's death.

Personal Application

YOU TOO MAY HAVE FELT WOUNDED, broken, powerless and incapable of helping yourself—or anyone else, for that matter. Your experiences in life can stymie you, stunt your growth and maturity, and make you bitter. Or they can mark you, mold you and make you into a better person.

The experiences you encounter on life's journey can serve as anchors that shape and ground you in preparation for challenges that lie ahead. As you deal with everyday annoyances and misunderstandings, your journey through life at times may seem difficult, or boring and mundane. Know that God is just as interested in the boring, mundane aspects of your life as he is in the big stuff. Regardless of your circumstances, God loves you more than you can possibly imagine.

Despite your troubles, God has promised never to leave you or forsake you. God may not take away your problems, but rest assured that he will help you make it through them. God is with you, perhaps even more during your crisis than at any other time. If you trust him, in his time, God can turn your pain and hardship into something meaningful.

If you are open to learning, your painful and perplexing situations can teach you important lessons. Identifying what you have learned through a hard or hurtful experience can actually bring dignity into the difficult or even ugly situation. Knowledge can be an amazing stepping-stone for growth and change. It can serve as a powerful catalyst to help you rise above the pot-holes of your circumstance. To begin a process of identifying your learnings, you can ask yourself:

- What have I learned about myself in this situation?
- What have I learned about others?

- What have I learned that can help me in the future?
- How would I handle myself in a similar situation?

Focusing on what you have learned takes your eyes off the negativity of your experience, and refocuses your attention on the positive. The choice to change your focus actually creates a shift in attitude, and that shift in attitude can be a powerful step in the process of healing. The wisdom you gain through difficult experiences will stand the test of time. Your learnings will serve as a foundation for your future, your choices and your healing.

....

EXPLORATION

1. Recall a personal storm in your life. Describe it. How did it happen and how did it affect you?

2. How did you respond to the storm?

3. How did you make it through?

4. What did you learn from that experience?

PRAYER

O God:

I know that storms are part of the journey of living. I feel like I am in a storm right now. At times the experience seems so dark and so severe I can't see where I'm going and I don't know where to turn. I need to know you are there. I desperately need your comfort and peace. I know you haven't caused my trials, but I do understand that you can use those experiences to help me grow. Quiet my heart, my head and my hands as I try to maneuver and manipulate the outcome. Stop my feet from running away from you. I believe you know what is best for me and you know the best path for me to take. I want to believe you can bring good out of bad. Please help me trust your ability. Teach me to see the things you want me to see, and to learn from those situations. Help me learn the things that are beyond my human ability to understand in this situation. Most of all, thank you for loving me in spite of my unbelief and my failings.

Amen.

CHAPTER: VII

BALANCE:

Meditation and pleasure brings strength and courage

IT is not the mountains we conquer, but ourselves.

—Sir Edmund Hillary

● ●

MY HUSBAND AND I ENJOY riding motorcycles. We have ridden as many as 12,000 miles during the biking season. Riding our motorcycles through God's beautiful creation is exhilarating. We spend long hours of solitude cruising scenic roads and mountain passes, relishing the sense of freedom that comes with the wind in our faces and the roar of our pipes.

"The more we appreciate life and experience joy, the better able we are to balance the pain and keep things in perspective," says the late Richard Carlson in his book, *What About the Big Stuff?* My motorcycle brings balance into my life. When I don my leathers and sit astride my iron horse, the stress of work and my busy life just melt away in the wind. On one long trip with a group of friends, my bike loaded with leather bags bulging with stuff I needed to stay warm and comfortable, we encountered a downpour. The heavy rain made the road look like a shimmering sheet of silver. We pulled into a filling station to put on rain gear.

Suited up and carefully backing my bike away from the curb, my left foot dropped into a hole full of rain, suddenly throwing me off balance. Try as I might, I couldn't keep my heavy bike upright. Right in front of my motorcycle friends I fell into the puddle—and a pool of humiliation. It must have been hilarious, watching me crawl out from under my bike, dripping wet. Fortunately, the only thing hurt was my pride, but that incident made me realize just how easy it is to become out of balance, and how we need help to stay upright.

On long rides it is my habit to focus my thoughts on God, on the attributes of his character. During these times instead of concentrating on a wish list of things I want God to do for me, I focus on who he is and how he reveals himself through those wonderful qualities I long for. Those extended periods of solitude on my bike have become a special time of worship. As I ride I create poetry, sing songs of praise and talk with God, friend to friend.

I also have a lot of fun on my bike. There is so much fun meeting new people, sharing times of laughter and beautiful places with our friends, feeling the surge of power as I throttle up, listening to the throbbing pipes as we ascend mountain passes.

I believe we become like those with whom we surround ourselves. Riding through the beauty of God's creation, experiencing it so intimately on my motorcycle, I imagine myself surrounded with God's loving presence. These times of motorcycle meditation take the focus off my problems and create an opportunity for thought, prayer, contemplation and wonderfully enriching experiences.

In the summer months after Soren died, my beautiful 1,500-cc cruiser became an instrument of healing. One day while riding a high mountain pass I chose to focus on the word courage. Little did I know the profound impact the word courage would have on me that day. Immersed in seeking a closer relationship with God, I prayed that his power would give me courage and release me from the wretched picture of Soren's death that continued to plague me. I also prayed for courage to face whatever personal mountains were in my future. I remember singing the song:

He is able, more than able to accomplish what concerns me today.
He is able, more than able to handle anything that comes my way.
He is able, more than able to do much more than I could ever dream.
He is able, more than able to make me what he wants me to be.

With that song I realized that the courage I needed was to allow God to control my affairs, to chart my future and create my healing. I realized that it takes courage to let go and let God do the fixing in his time and in his way.

Ascending the mountain pass was challenging and exhilarating. I leaned into the curves, gearing down to maneuver in safety and gearing up again on the straight stretches. I loved feeling my powerful machine pulling me effortlessly up the steep slopes, the deep, rich sound of my exhaust pipes barking against the craggy cliffs and echoing in the canyons. I kept close behind my husband, our bikes creating a rhythmic harmony as we rode in close succession.

Mountains have always intrigued me and have been symbolic in my life. On mountain roads brakes can fail, and a misjudged curve can send a motorcyclist careening off into space or headlong into oncoming traffic. Though not a mountain climber, I enjoy the mountains in other ways. They are not only majestic and full of wonder, they are ever-changing as the sun and moon illuminate their surfaces and create mysterious shadows. Mountains are full of challenge and danger. Mountains beg to be climbed, and the view from the top brings perspective. This is not unlike the mountains we face in traveling life's journey. William Blake said, "Great things are done when men and mountains meet." Focusing on the courage of God, I quickly realized that I didn't know the mind of God. In my own limited understanding, I could only imagine the courage it took to send his Son to earth for our benefit, but even more than that, the courage it must have taken to watch from a distance as his Son hung on the cross as a sacrifice for the entire human race.

Right there on my bike, pondering the courage of Jesus Christ as he faced his accusers and the mob that despised him and then surged forward as a group to crucify him, I couldn't hold back the tears. He had no one to rescue him from the torment he chose to endure on our behalf. Fully grasping the enormity of what Jesus had done, knowing that he had done it for me personally, was an amazing experience. I must admit my own personal level of courage seemed puny in comparison to the courage I had just contemplated of our God and Savior.

As we climbed higher and higher, navigating switchbacks and hairpin curves, I changed my focus to praying for the courage to maneuver my motorcycle safely and to remain alert, vigilant and conscious of the danger lurking around each bend. I knew God was my riding companion, and he would help me make wise riding decisions that would enable me to reach the summit.

Sure enough, soon I could see the summit. What a magnificent sight! We had conquered the mountain on our motorcycles, and we were on top of the world. The glistening sun, the clear blue sky and the cool wind on my face gave me a joy I can't describe. Looking up, I saw the most magnificent eagle. Circling, soaring and climbing into the heavens with grace and ease, floating effortlessly above the highest peak, the eagle seemed to me to be a symbol of the freedom, the strength and even the peace I could receive from God. Watching the eagle soaring high above me, in the depths of my being I heard a strong yet gentle voice. *"If you wait on me, you will find new strength and you will rise up on wings like eagles." (Isaiah 40:31).* I was amazed by the words I had just heard. The message was so clear. To get my attention, God had used an eagle as a messenger. I knew I had received a message meant just for me. All the way down the other side of the mountain, I pondered and processed what I had just experienced.

It was like God was saying, "Annette, just wait. I will give you courage in a way, and at a time, when you need it. If you trust me I will carry you and give you a freedom you've never known before. Let my wings be the wings that give you strength, courage and freedom." Wow! What an amazing experience. I'd read that passage many times, but this time it was as if God was giving me a fresh lesson—a lesson that filled me with hope that he would provide the courage I had been praying for.

I didn't have any idea what the future might hold, or what it might be about. But now I had the calm assurance that God would carry me; that something wonderful would happen to fill me with strength and freedom beyond my understanding. I knew I would be able to rise above any trial or storm that lay ahead.

PERSONAL APPLICATION

THE MESSAGE THE EAGLE BROUGHT to me on the mountain was so powerful that my husband and I have created an eagle's nest in our home. A relaxing room containing beautiful eagle pictures, figurines, a waterfall and foliage, it reminds us of being on a mountain top with eagles soaring above us. In that special place we study, pray, talk and meditate about things that will help us climb the personal mountains we face.

Situations in your own life may seem like mountains. These can be big, frightening, formidable circumstances looming in your path, or they can be events, relationships, wounds and conditions that seem insurmountable. It is easy to focus all your attention on these situations, and to lose the ability to enjoy life. Your problems, discouragements and disappointments can totally consume you. If you allow that to happen, however, you can lose your balance.

Attempting to regain equilibrium, it is easy to become fixated on the "if onlys." If only she hadn't; if only he would; if only I could; if only they weren't.... The list of "if onlys" can go on and on. But that's a trap. Don't attempt to blame circumstances or other people for what is wrong in your life. Tough stuff happens! No amount of "if onlys" will change what has happened.

The actions or omissions of others often make us feel like we've been victimized or that our life is always someone else's fault. "They" did this thing. "They" prevented me from getting ahead. "They" wouldn't let me..... and the victimhood list goes on and on, creating a mindset that circles downward into the miry quicksand of stuckness.

Unmet expectations are another common trap. When you create your own set of rules about how life should happen, you often find that other people do not measure up. When your rules and expectations are not met, you become angry and disappointed.

Rules for life are actually unenforceable, because you cannot force your own list of rules on anyone else. When you obsess about unmet expectations, you can reach a point where you can't move beyond the picture of your own unenforceable rules. Focusing on your own self-centeredness, and criticizing others, simply increases your imbalance.

If you've ever been dizzy, you'll understand what I mean. When your equilibrium is impaired, you run into walls and doors. You find it difficult to stand up straight. You just want to lie down, close your eyes and hope the imbalance will go away.

It takes courage to face your problems. One way of regaining balance is to refocus. If you take the focus off yourself and how you've been hurt, disappointed or misjudged, and refocus your attention on what you can do to improve the matter, you will regain balance. In turn, balance will help you navigate the path leading to your own well-being.

EXPLORATION

1. Think about a mountain or an obstacle in your life that makes you feel anxious, afraid, out of balance or even powerless.

2. Reflect on a situation you just can't seem to fix.

   How does that situation make you feel?

3. What characteristics do you need most to help you cope with a mountain you're facing in your life?

4. How can you gain those qualities that could make a difference in the situation?

PRAYER

O God:

Thank you for helping me understand the mountains in my life.
I know there are scary situations that I am afraid to face. There are
circumstances where my strength and courage are weak. I know I
am afraid of those situations. Thank you for promising to give me
courage and strength, and for promising that you will always
be with me, helping me over the mountains in my life.

God, I particularly need your help in my situation with (name
a situation you are struggling with). Teach me to lean on you and
help me to be open to placing my trust in your ability to carry
me. Teach me to be patient and to keep you as my climbing
companion. I want to learn to rely on your strength, courage
and wisdom to face those things that are holding me back.
Thank you for promising that you will always be there
with me, and that you will give me wisdom.

Amen.

CHAPTER: VIII

ACCEPTANCE:
The puzzle unravels

ACCEPTANCE is essential for healing and crucial for transformation.

—Annette Stanwick

• •

F OR MORE THAN A YEAR after Soren's death we had no answers about who had taken his life. Even though my grief was always just under the surface, life resumed a semblance of normalcy. I became resigned to the fact that we might never know who had killed my brother.

One day a call came from the FBI agent investigating the case. The FBI had arrested three brothers along with their mother and a cousin from Virginia for conspiring to steal a big truck. A trucker was killed during the incident. Along with some other episodes of stolen trucks, there was reason to believe that the same people were responsible for Soren's death. Overwhelmed by the information, once again I was catapulted back into horrendous pain. "Serial killers!"

flashed through my mind. I felt as though another storm had hit my life. A tornado of emotions and grief tossed me about, wrenching me from the stable ground I thought I stood on. I was hurled right back into the middle of the ugly picture—only this time the picture had more frames.

That a mother and her three sons had concocted this astonishing plan was especially sordid and unbelievable. A third trucker left for dead had apparently survived. I shared shreds of this with my husband and our daughters, but I couldn't bear to repeat the details to anyone else.

"I want to ride," I said, knowing that I needed to spend some time in solitude with God, hoping that the blue sky and open road would filter out all the horrible thoughts whirling in my mind, that the warmth of the summer sun and the luscious scenery would calm my tangled nerves.

Clay and I joined a group of friends from our Christian Motorcyclists' Association on a short run into the country. None of them knew the most recent development. I couldn't talk about the unspeakable details we'd just been given.

I selected the word "acceptance" for my focus that morning. I had no idea where that word might take me. As we rode through the countryside, we passed beautiful meandering wheat fields framed by acres of grassland that literally came alive with patches of brilliant yellow canola in full bloom. As we rode, I reflected on God's unconditional acceptance of us, regardless of who we are and what we've done. His type of acceptance is astonishing, almost unbelievable. I began praising God and thanking him for his acceptance of me in the past, when I had hurt him and disappointed him terribly, even when I had lashed out at him in rage when I first learned of Soren's death.

I knew that to accept the horrible picture of my brother's murder, a picture that suddenly had become clearer, I needed

God's help. I had wanted answers, even prayed for them, but now that I had some of those answers I didn't want to deal with the information. "God, I'm struggling to accept what I've just learned," I prayed. "I know that to move on I have to accept the facts, but it all seems too ugly to believe. Please help me."

My relationship with God had deepened in the months after Soren's death. I was confident in my connection with him. Never did I doubt that God had spoken to me in the hospital after my head-on collision, or in the middle of the night after Soren died, or on my motorcycle on the summit of the mountain.

Many of my friends have asked, "How do you know God is the one speaking to you?" It's a reasonable question. What makes me recognize God's voice?

The Bible says that God speaks to those who believe in him. When you've heard him speak to you in a very profound way, you recognize his voice. We can hear his message through the things we read in the Bible, through nature, through an audible voice, through our conscience and through impressions on our heart.

There is no doubt in my mind that God was the one speaking to me, in the instances I've listed and on many other occasions as well. Those experiences have been so profound I can't fully describe the effect they have had on me.

A friend once said, "Annette, it seems like your life is full of miracles and times when God speaks." I must admit that it does feel like a miracle when things happen that are far beyond anyone's ability to orchestrate. Events have happened that I have no other way of explaining except that they are miracles, or divine appointments, or God's voice.

On one occasion, I was playing the piano very late at night when I had the sudden urge to call a friend in another province, where the time was even later. I got up in the middle of a measure of music and called my friend. She wasn't home, but her husband answered the phone. After a few moments of conversation he confessed that he was sitting at a table with a gun pointed at his head, ready to pull the trigger. My friend had left him, and he was devastated by the loss of their marriage.

I spent a long time talking with him, encouraging him and helping him through his crisis. I was astounded by that experience. I'll never forget it. Only God could have urged me to call at that critical instant.

I believe God wants everyone to hear his voice, but we need to listen, recognize and acknowledge that it is God who is speaking to us. We also need to respond to the love, encouragement, caution and direction he gives. A relationship with God is not just head knowledge and book learning. A personal relationship with God, the creator of the universe, is experiential, real and heart-changing.

As we rode through the fresh, green countryside, tears of anguish were streaming down my face as I thought about the information the FBI had given our family. In an impetuous, reckless moment I cranked open the throttle of my motorcycle. Passing everyone in our group, racing down the highway as fast as my bike would go, it was as if I had to rid myself of the pent-up emotion. Over and over I asked, "Why Soren? Why did they kill Soren?"

Imagining the horror of Soren's last moments as he was assaulted, beaten and shot in the cab of his truck by three brothers, I asked God if there was something I still needed to learn. My pain was so deep that I cried out in the wind as I rode, literally throttling my way through the pain.

I realized I wasn't handling myself—or the bike—very well. After several miles of throbbing pipes and torrents of tears, I began to slow down so the rest of our group could catch up. As I slowed, God gave me an answer, and a recipe to begin healing.

An image of three crosses appeared in my mind's eye. This image was as clear as if I'd been transported back in time to that dreadful day when Jesus was crucified on the cross of Calvary. With those three crosses looming before me, a voice spoke the same words that Jesus spoke as he hung on the cross. Even though I'd heard those words many times, this time they were spoken directly to me. The voice said, "Forgive them; for they know not what they do."

I couldn't believe what I had just heard. "Forgive them; for they know not what they do."

I repeated the last part of that statement—"they know not what they do."

Soren's killers didn't know what they were doing. I finally had an answer to my question. It was crystal clear. They didn't know what they were doing. They didn't even know my brother!

The family who did this despicable thing didn't know how much Soren was loved, how much he would be missed, or how much he was needed. This horrible act was not against him, the person. Their violence wasn't because they hated him. They wanted his truck, and he stood in the way, so they killed him.

In one swift moment I had found the answer to the question that had plagued me for over a year. Even though the picture that had been painted was still difficult to look at, that answer brought relief. But now I had to deal with the rest of the message.

"Forgive them." Forgive them! "No! No! No!" I screamed. As I rode, I sensed another wrestling match beginning. I struggled with the thoughts racing through my mind. "I can't do it! Don't ask me to forgive them. It doesn't make sense. They murdered my brother! Please, no! Don't expect this of me."

Again I heard God's voice. "Forgive and you will be forgiven. Forgive as I have forgiven you." It was a clear call to obedience that could not be denied. "Oh God, how can I do this?" I sobbed. "I can't possibly forgive. It hurts so much to know the pain and terror he went through. They deserve to die, and you ask me to forgive them. I can't forgive!"

Again the voice spoke, and this time it was very personal. "Annette, my strength is sufficient for you. I didn't come to condemn. I came to give life and to give life abundantly. I will uphold you, and when you forgive as you have been forgiven, you will rise up as on eagle's wings."

I couldn't argue anymore. I couldn't struggle. I wasn't being forced, but I was being pointed in a direction by the loving, gentle voice I knew so well. It was a voice of love telling me that his strength was enough to help me do what I thought was impossible. God was promising that I would be forgiven, and that I would rise above this situation.

When the creator of the universe speaks and you hear his voice above the rumble of your motorcycle pipes and the wild beating of your heart, you know you're in God's presence, and you know he means every word.

Exhausted when we arrived at our destination, I couldn't speak of my experience. It was too fresh, too emotional, too overwhelming. The little town we had come to was hosting an outdoor car show. Gleaming automobiles and trucks, restored, re-upholstered and repainted in luxurious colors, made the streets glint as though studded with brilliant jewels. Off to one side was a display of big trucks, polished to perfection. Every piece of gleaming chrome you could imagine glistened in the sun.

Alone, immersed in the world of trucking, my eyes landed on a truck that took my breath away—a Western Star just like the one Soren drove, painted the very same color. Staring through the window, imagining the struggle inside Soren's truck the day he died, I began to sob uncontrollably. As I wept, I pondered the extraordinary experience that morning on my motorcycle. I was at an important crossroads. With the picture of Soren's death re-opened, the grief had returned. And now, layered on top, was the knowledge that God was asking to me to forgive.

I needed to make a choice. Which road would I take? Would I go down the path that would take me away from what I perceived to be God's will? I could easily go that way—no one else knew about the experience on my bike that morning. But if I took that direction I would be walking away from the one who understood my pain, the one who understood forgiveness. That path would never lead to the peace I longed for. Instead, it would leave me plagued with guilt for ignoring the voice of God.

On the other hand, the road to forgiveness was frightening. I didn't know how to do what God was asking of me. I didn't know if I could forgive. Where would that road lead?

"I want to do your will," I prayed, "but I don't know how to forgive such a terrible thing. If forgiving my brother's murderers is what you want me to do, then you will have to make it possible."

With a heavy sigh, I stopped for a silent moment of submission and surrender. I knew that God would be with me. He would give me the strength I needed. He had given me strength in the past, so I knew I could trust him. Finally, I realized I had made my choice.

PERSONAL APPLICATION

WE WOULD ALL LIKE OUR PAINFUL PAST to go away, to be able to push the delete button on the keyboard of our lives. But life isn't like that. You have to deal with stuff, or it comes back to haunt you.

Acceptance is an important step in dealing with the stuff. It is a vital part of the grieving and healing process. Acceptance is at the heart of transformation. Your role is to acknowledge and accept what has happened.

Fighting a negative situation expends precious energy pushing back against a reality you cannot change anyway. Fighting the negative keeps you bound. It keeps you circling round and round in anger at the circumstances.

Roger John said, "When you are in a state of nonacceptance, it's difficult to learn. A clenched fist cannot receive a gift, and a clenched psyche cannot easily receive a lesson."

Acceptance frees you to take positive steps toward recovery, change and growth. It actually refocuses your energy in an affirmative direction of forward movement. Acceptance does not mean defeat. It means standing on the step of acknowledgment ready to move to the next phase. What is past is past. You cannot turn back the clock. To move on, you need to accept what has happened. Only when you acknowledge and accept the fact that you cannot change the past, will you be able to move to the next step— seeking the courage to change the things you can.

What can you change? You can change your response to what has happened. Instead of being a victim, you can seek help in becoming a survivor. You need to ask yourself what part you are playing in keeping yourself stuck in suffering.

Your experience of responding to the situation is totally in your hands. Progress in the journey of healing is fully your choice.

Change your attitude. Instead of wallowing in pity, ask what you can learn from this situation. How can you grow and change? How can you prevent this from happening again? How can you prevent it from happening to others? How can you help others move forward in their own worlds of pain?

. . . .

EXPLORATION

1. What part of your story or experience do you have difficulty accepting?

   Describe your difficulty.

2. What is it that you cannot change about the situation? (Be clear and specific.)

3. What is within the scope of your personal power to change?

4. What help do you need in making changes?

5. Who can help you?

PRAYER

O God:

Quiet my mind and my heart from the painful pictures and memories I continue to relive. Help me to focus my thoughts on how you would want me to respond to the situation of (be specific). Help me to feel your acceptance of me, regardless of what I've been like in the past. Show me those things that are keeping me stuck. I need you to help me identify and accept the things I cannot change. Help me to know if they are keeping me stuck. Help me to see those things that I can change. I long to sense your presence in my life. Open my ears and my heart that I might hear your voice speaking to my heart. Please help me learn the things you want to teach me. I need your strength, as I work through these important issues in my life.

Amen.

CHAPTER: IX

LETTING GO:
Essential ingredient in healing

FAITH believes God and his word when,
circumstances, emotions, appearances,
people and human reason all seem to urge
something to the contrary.

—L.B. Cowan

··

NOT LONG AFTER MY WILD MOTORCYCLE RIDE with God
I received a call from Starli advising me that Travis, one
of the three brothers, had confessed to pulling the trigger in
Soren's death. He was the second oldest. Because of his confession,
Travis would not stand trial for his offense but would no doubt
be sentenced to life in prison.

Starli asked if I would like to attend his sentencing in Richmond,
Virginia. I immediately said yes. I wanted to see the person who
had stolen my brother's life.

Then Starli asked another question. She asked if I wanted to
present a Victim Impact Statement.

At the time, I had no inkling of the momentous implications of that question, or my answer. I had no idea what a Victim Impact Statement was. Nevertheless, without hesitation I said, "Yes!"

With several months before the day of sentencing, I had time to consider the matter. In my research I learned that the family member of the victim normally reads a statement to the accused in front of the judge just prior to sentencing. The statement tells the accused how the crime affected the victim or victim's family. My mind flooded with all the things I could say. I collected a list of everything I wanted to communicate, things that would paint a verbal picture for Travis of the pain that Soren's death had caused.

A friend invited me to join a small writing group for women. We met every two weeks to write and discuss what we had written about our perspectives on various topics. That writing group became an important means of helping me in the healing process. It motivated me to continue writing, and my writing became a powerful tool for exploring and expressing my thoughts on paper. Through my writing, I began to more clearly understand my feelings, emotions, fears, revelations and even transformations.

As the time drew near to leave for the sentencing, I spent hours on the computer, crafting the thoughts I wanted to deliver in the courtroom. After printing off a copy, I moved to the living room, the beautiful CD *His Love* by Debra Zahar playing softly in the background. I read and reread my graphic description of what the murder had done to me, and to my family. Overwhelmed with the deep wounds, with the sense of loss and sadness that Soren's death had created, my tears flowed and my body trembled with weakness. It seemed like my heart was empty. It felt broken.

I remember whispering to God that the pain and sorrow were so deep I could barely move. I could not seem to escape the darkness surrounding me. It felt like I was in a black hole, with no way to escape. I pleaded for God's presence to wash over me, to heal me and to help me release my thoughts, feelings and sorrows into his loving hands. In the background, the beautiful song *In His Presence* was playing softly. The second verse was personal.

In your presence there is comfort
In your presence there is peace.
When we seek to know your heart,
We will find such blessed assurance
In your holy presence, Lord.

I sensed God's presence surrounding me and comforting me. In my writing I had fully faced and embraced my brokenness, and now I was surrendering that brokenness to God. He was doing his work. I sat there for several hours, unable to move, praying, allowing the tears to flow and listening to healing songs about God's love and sacrifice.

As I sat, I realized that my struggle to forgive was not with God. I felt his soothing presence all around me. My struggle was with me. I realized that God was giving his gift of forgiveness to me. Forgiveness is about letting go! Forgiveness is about releasing and relinquishing all those things that we hold onto. I had been holding onto the wound. I hadn't let go of the hurt and anger. I hadn't released my feelings and emotions, my losses and grief. It was all still right there, in my tight tormented fists of control.

Opening my tightly closed hands, I began physically relinquishing my stronghold on pain, grief and anger. In my writing I had graphically faced the pain, and now I was physically releasing everything to God. It felt as though I was abandoning myself.

When I finally let go, releasing my heart into the hands of God, a sense of comfort poured over me. The freedom and peace I experienced through that act of surrender was like nothing else I had ever experienced. What a gift! In the calm, quiet moment of surrender, God was finally able to do his work in me. I knew with absolute certainty what I had to do. But I couldn't do it alone. To deliver my message in the courtroom, I needed God's help. I knew I could trust him because he was the one who had commanded me to deliver that message.

I also realized I needed the support, prayers and encouragement of my family and friends who had stood beside me throughout the grieving process. I have always been strong and independent, rarely asking for help in times of need, but this was somehow different. Two days before we left for Virginia, I called a group of friends together.

The friends who came that night represented a cross-section of our lives. Although they had different backgrounds, professions and religious affiliations, they had all touched me personally during my time of grief. Many didn't know each other. None of them knew the message I was going to deliver.

Sitting in my living room, I gave them a capsule view of the journey I'd been on. I asked them to hear my message, and to pray for me as we traveled to Virginia and as I spoke to Travis in the courtroom. After I read my Victim Impact Statement they knelt around me, praying to help me find the faith I needed for what God was asking me to do. What strength and encouragement I received that night! I could barely speak when the evening ended and everyone left. The next day my executive colleagues at work also tenderly prayed for me in the boardroom, and that was another experience I'll never forget.

When our extended family converged in Richmond, the tension and fear we felt was palpable. Over the next two days we would come face to face with the facts—and with the person who had caused us so much pain over the past nineteen months.

Our visit was carefully arranged by the FBI under the direction of the lead investigator assigned to Soren's case in cooperation with the federal prosecutor. We visited the crime scene and learned details we hadn't known. We met the federal prosecutor who prepared us for the proceedings in court the next day.

We also met a gentle, aging African American trucker who Soren's assailants had badly injured and left for dead. As we listened to him describe his torment, we each held him in our arms and wept. Later, my brother Chris said that listening to him describe what had happened felt as though we were entering into Soren's pain.

The family of another trucker killed by Travis and his brothers was so traumatized they were unable to face the situation. They did not present Victim Impact Statements.

At FBI headquarters we listened to investigators carefully presenting the details of the case and tactfully answering our questions. Larry, the lead investigator, had a large picture of Soren on his bulletin board with a caption that read, "Lest we forget." He truly saw Soren as a person, not just a statistic. It was clear that he had been relentless in pursuing details to solve this mystery. We saw a side of the FBI not often portrayed on television—a group of kind, caring investigators who were truly committed to solving crimes that victimize people.

Prior to arriving in Virginia I had called to request that all police, ambulance and autopsy records along with photos of the crime be made available. The prosecutor and investigator discouraged us from viewing the photos, trying to protect us from unnecessary pain, knowing those dreaded images would become seared in our memories. Taking the lead, I repeated my request. I wanted the photos and records to be available. I believed we had the right to choose whether we viewed them.

The rest of my family agreed. We sat at a large conference table passing the documents around. We each had the opportunity to read every report, and scouring those documents helped us understand what Soren had endured. I was able to interpret many of the medical facts and terms. In the autopsy findings, I clearly saw that Soren had fought hard for his life. His body and internal organs were badly bruised before the two fateful shots ended his life. Soren was a strong, powerful man, quick on his feet and quick in his reactions. Being a Vietnam war veteran, he knew how to use his body and his might to fight. It was no surprise to see clearly that he had fought hard to ward off the attacks of those three men determined to steal his truck.

In a strong gesture of compassion and protection, my husband viewed the photos first, in private. "They're hard to look at," he said quietly. "It's up to you."

I had traveled all the way from Calgary to have as many questions answered as possible. I was afraid to look at the pictures, but I also knew that I needed to face my fear. I didn't want to have regrets and I didn't want to be stuck. Choosing to continue the healing process, I asked to see the photos. Clay accompanied me to the other end of the table. I sat with my back to the others so no one would see my face. Silent tears fell as I carefully examined each image. When I finished, I laid the package in front of them.

"The pictures aren't nice," I said. "They are very graphic, very real, and very hard to look at. But nothing for me could be worse than seeing Soren's dead body in that casket. I've had many questions answered by these pictures. In some cases, my imagination was worse than the reality. Each of you must make your own choice."

Most chose to view everything. Facing the facts together as a family strengthened us individually. We are grateful we made the choice that day to face our fears. It helped us each move on.

That night in our room Clay was tender and thoughtful. "After what you've seen and heard today," he asked, "how do you feel about what you will say in the courtroom tomorrow?"

"I am prepared," I replied calmly, "and I know God will be with me." Despite my trepidation, I slept well that night.

The next morning our seventeen family members met in the hotel lobby. I could sense each person's anxiety. Today we would see Travis for the first time, and ten of us would present Victim Impact Statements. Walking the two blocks to the courthouse we talked little, each person engrossed in thought, then filed into the courtroom that soon began to fill.

I was afraid of what I would experience when I saw Travis. Would I be repulsed? Would I change my mind? My family did not know what I was about to say. How would they respond? How would Travis respond?

We sat in silence, awaiting the arrival of my brother's murderer. As we sat, the sun began shining through the window and an incredible peace came over me. I felt as though a host of angels was surrounding me. The stream of sunlight on my face seemed like God's love shining directly on me.

The double doors of the courtroom suddenly opened. The crowd became silent. In walked Travis. Every eye went to the man who had taken Soren's life. Wearing a prison jumpsuit, Travis shuffled forward with his head down, his feet shackled and his hands cuffed behind his back. The haunting sound of his chains and leg irons pierced the quiet of the courtroom.

I stared at the man who had destroyed a home and wounded our hearts. What did I see? I saw a good-looking young man accused, alone, afraid and ashamed. I also saw a young man who I knew God loved, in spite of what he had done.

We listened intently to a tale of twenty-five years of emotional abuse and unfaithfulness inflicted by Travis's father on his wife and three sons. We learned of the loneliness and lack of role modeling experienced by the brothers. We heard of the poverty and shame within their home, and in their community. It was obvious that the entire family was wounded. As I listened, I felt compassion for them in spite of what they had done to Soren and others.

Their wounds didn't give license to what they had done, but I could sense how the abandonment and abuse had contributed to the life those young men had embraced.

One by one, ten broken-hearted members of our family spoke of their own pain, anger spewing out of their mouths and tears tumbling from their eyes. The courtroom became filled with emotion. As the oldest, having shared life with Soren the longest, I would be the last to speak. The time for my Victim Impact Statement was approaching. I was about to experience the biggest test of my life.

....

Personal Application

PERHAPS YOU HAVE NEVER REALLY ADDRESSED a painful experience. Just thinking about the situation may cause you to feel tense, angry, afraid or resentful. These thoughts cause your muscles and gut to tighten. They make your heart race and your palms sweat. Thoughts of what someone has done to you may make you want to run and hide, or to lash out and hurt that person. The thoughts may even catapult you back into the memory. You may feel the same physical and emotional pain you experienced at the time of your wounding.

These flashbacks are called Post Traumatic Stress Disorder (PTSD). If you experience PTSD flashbacks and nightmares, be gentle with yourself. The pain and the memories will eventually subside. It helps if you logically reason with yourself that the person cannot hurt you right at this moment.

Remembering what has happened can be frightening. You may not want to focus on the person or event. But if you are able to focus on the impact of that person, or that event, it can help a great deal in your healing process. Identifying and giving your pain a voice can be therapeutic. Embracing the pain for what it is—hurtful, ugly, and destructive is facing it, walking through it and then leaving it there. Release and let go of the stronghold those feelings have on you. Releasing and letting go will help bring healing.

EXPLORATION

1. What did that person do to me, or to the person I love?

2. How did it make me feel?

3. How did it make me feel about myself?

4. How does it make me feel about others?

5. How does it affect how I relate to other people?

6. How does it affect my family and our relationships?

7. What have I learned through that experience?

PRAYER

O God:

I am afraid of confronting how I feel about the person who hurt me. It is even difficult to describe how I feel. I am afraid of losing control. I've stuffed my feelings for so long that I've tried to believe they no longer exist, yet I know they are still there. Open my heart and my mind so I can identify why I feel so hurt, so violated and even so ashamed. Help me to be compassionate with myself. I need to know that it is okay to feel anger, bitterness and even hatred for what has happened. But please don't leave me there in that place of pain. Help me to trust that you can help me in walking through this frightening experience. Thank you for your patience and understanding. Thank you for loving me just the way I am, but also for not wanting to leave me the way I am.

Amen.

CHAPTER: X

FORGIVENESS:
Telling the story face to face

SHARING your feelings with someone
who is listening is important even if your
emotion causes the anger to reappear
and the tears to flow.

—Dr. Phil McGraw

· ·

IN THE WITNESS STAND I turned to look directly at Travis. For the first time, our eyes locked. I paused for a moment, praying for courage and strength. After taking a deep breath, I began to speak. Methodically and precisely I described the pictures I wanted Travis and the judge to see—pictures about our family, and of the impact Soren's death had on us.

A hush fell over the room. Unaware of anything but the message I was delivering to Travis, to the judge, to my family members and to the spectators in the courtroom, I slowly and carefully began describing our torment and suffering. Here, word for word, is what I said.

VICTIM IMPACT STATEMENT
Annette Stanwick

Accused:
Travis Friend
24 October 2000
Richmond, Virginia

I want to begin by saying how grateful I am to the Justice System of Virginia for making it possible for me to be here today to describe for you the impact that the intentional and violent murder of my brother Soren has had on my family and me.

To begin my statement, I would like to create a picture of my family and in particular, the relationship I had with my brother Soren.

My name is Annette Cornforth Stanwick. I am the only daughter and the oldest of four children in my family. Soren Cornforth was my oldest brother, just five years and three months younger than me.

At a very young age I took on a parental role for my three brothers. Due to the ill health of my mother, before and after the birth of my two younger brothers, along with three simultaneous accidental deaths in my mother's family, I was called upon to care for my brothers. I dressed them, fed them, played with them and even disciplined them while my mother was nursing her own wounded heart and tired mind and body. There were times when the entire responsibilities of mothering my three brothers seemingly fell on my shoulders.

In carrying out that role from such a young age, I believe the heart attachment, deep love and strong bond with Soren and my two younger brothers, Chris and Rick, seemed deeper than that of a sister. I loved them and cherished them with a love that cannot be fully understood.

My family is a loving, caring, responsible, community-oriented family. We were taught Christian values, along with a fun-loving, free-spirited love for life and a love for people. And we all possess a deep desire to make a difference wherever we go or whatever we're involved in. Our family's whole existence and philosophy of life has been built on love and caring and the value of the human spirit. While Soren wasn't perfect, his life and character was a strong portrayal of those family values deeply engrained in each of us.

Our family has bonds that can never be broken though the years and miles may separate us. Family events were always wonderful occasions for joy, fun, frolic and countless telling and retelling, living and reliving of memories. Now our story telling for generations to come will be punctuated with the unbelievable story of Soren's murder.

This dreadful drama began for me on the morning of March 1, 1999, when my youngest brother, Rick, called to tell me of Soren's death. Rick was experiencing so much grief and pain he could barely whisper the words, "Soren has been murdered."

Murder doesn't happen in our family. It is unimaginable, incomprehensible and even outlandish to even entertain the thought that someone could be so callus, cruel or capable of intentionally killing my brother, MY BROTHER! The excruciating pain at hearing those unbelievable words was almost more than I could bear. The indescribable, deep, agonizing, gut-wrenching sounds of anguish could not be quelled as my body, mind and soul were wracked with the instancy of overwhelming grief and sorrow.

I will never forget the deep, searing, tissue-ripping pain in my chest that felt like my heart was being ripped right out of my body. My husband, Clayton, and my youngest daughter, Shelann, almost seemed to be in a shocked paralysis as they tried to comfort me while witnessing the moments of horror and grief being played out in the reality of our home.

My oldest daughter, Mona, was alone, grief-stricken and angry when she learned of her uncle's death. One shouldn't be alone when learning of such news. In her role as a corrections officer, Mona frequently supervises and works with murderers. As a result of her uncle's death, she began to see each murderer she works with in the light of the horror that you and your brothers created for an uncle she loved so much, Travis.

Travis, with this hideous act, you have suddenly thrust my entire family into the middle of a murder mystery. We find ourselves, our emotions, our fears, our imaginations and our grief played out on each page as this incredible story unravels.

We just barely seem to regain some equilibrium when a new chapter opens or some new information emerges and we are then catapulted back into the pain of this real life drama that we can't escape from. Yes, you created a murder mystery, Travis, and furthermore, you wrote it about my brother, Soren, and you wrote it with his precious blood.

The vivid realism of that hideous true story is also played out in full life-sized color on the personal memory screens of all of us who are before you today, as well as countless others who could not be here. And that movie goes into instant replay anytime, day or night without warning, just by the trigger of a thought, a sight, a sound or a feeling.

Travis, the impact of Soren's murder has:

1. Left our relationship with Soren frozen in time. Some wish they could turn back the clock and undo things that were said or done or to make amends where there may have been misunderstandings or injured feelings, or even just to say, "I'm sorry."

2. Robbed us of the opportunity to tell him one more time how much we love him, need him and value him.

3. Chained us to the incredible visions and nightmares of horror he must have experienced in the last few moments of his life.

4. Prevented us from experiencing a complete life with Soren. This random act of violence has literally ripped him out of our family picture.

5. Left our mother grief-stricken, bereft and in anguish as she forever ponders the unanswered question of WHY?

6. Brutally stolen from my two wonderful daughters the future of enjoying the laughter, lighthearted, free-spirited, fun-loving antics of an uncle they loved to be near. His spontaneity and maverick ways were so full of life and fun and the way in which he teased my daughters created moments they will miss forever.

7. Carelessly shattered one of the spokes in our family wheel, leaving a void and a weakness that will forever be noticed as we roll through life together.

8. Left some family members unable to process this whole horrid picture or even to begin to identify or unravel their own feelings as a result of what this means and how their own future and the future of their family will be affected.

9. Caused us to be fearful in society where once we were pillars of courage and trust.

10. Left us constantly trying to imagine Soren's last word, last thoughts, his fear, his terror, his valiant struggle to save his own life and even his probable frantic cry for help.

11. Soren's murder has torn the innocence from our circle of family love, leaving a deep, dark, cavernous wound that will forever weep and ooze with tears.

My brother wasn't perfect, but I loved him so much. I was proud of him and we had a good relationship.

He took such pride in his big truck and it was so much fun to have him take me on a demonstration ride through the country, showing me how he could maneuver his mighty machine through the highways and cities of America. But that truck became his death trap when he couldn't escape the cowardly intruders intent on taking his life. I am a strong woman, but the senseless, selfish acts of violence that ended my brother's life have scarred my own heart and emotions so deeply that I need professional help to cope with his death.

- I thought I was losing my mind.

- I saw perfectly normal looking men as murderers, and men not to be trusted.

- When out in public I wanted to shout to the world, "Stop, don't you know my brother has been murdered?"

- I searched the faces of each trucker I passed, hoping beyond hope I would once again see the handsome, smiling face of my brother Soren at the controls of the truck I was passing.

- I wept in my pillow night after night as my heart longed to reach out to him and make him live again.

- I've ached to hear the sounds of his voice, his laughter, and his poetry.

- I've stared for hours on end at his picture, trying desperately to imagine him moving through life, recalling the moments we've shared and the sounds of his voice as we laughed, cried and relived life's experiences together.

- I've longed to hear his voice on the phone, teasing, jesting and creating moments of fun and laugher.

- I miss the tender moments of sharing and deep discussions we had long into the night after everyone else had gone to bed. It was then that the masks would come off and we could be real with each other, sharing some of the deep pain, fears, disappointments and insecurities as well as the joys and the triumphs of our lives.

- I miss the beautiful and thoughtful prayers he would offer as we would leave his home to return to our home in Canada.

- It created unbelievable sadness and pain to know that a brother I loved so much was helplessly victimized and murdered.

- It is unfathomable for me to even consider the notion that the ultimate atrocity of taking his life could be necessary for a few measly possessions.

In spite of the pain and sorrow of the past nineteen months and the journey of recovering from such a terrible loss, there are some important things I have learned throughout this whole experience.

Travis, it is only through God's goodness, his tender love and care and the unconditional love and forgiveness he has so graciously given to me, that I am now able to look at you through eyes that see beyond the hideous thing you did in killing my brother. What I am about to say will never erase or excuse what you have done to Soren.

What I am about to say, however, does come from the very depths of my soul. The following thoughts come from hours of tearful prayer and contemplation and from God's Spirit making impressions on my heart. Travis, I believe that you have a deeply wounded heart, or you would never have been able to do what you did to Soren. You:

- Didn't know him

- Didn't know his name

- Didn't know how much he was loved

- Didn't know how much he was needed

- Didn't know how much he would be missed

- Didn't know what a contribution he had made and still could make in his community, in his family and in his world.

Travis, I believe you didn't know who my brother was. I also believe your violent act was not against him, the person, Soren. I believe your act of violence was out of fear and deep need and Soren stood in the way of what you needed, so you made a choice, and that choice was to take his life. Our family is now left to cope with the tragic and unforgettable results of your choice for the rest of our lives and you must now suffer the consequences of that choice for the rest of your life.

Travis, I want you to know that the most important impact of this whole experience for me is that God has given me a new understanding of love and forgiveness.

Travis, God has impressed me that:

- He doesn't love what you did, but he loves you in spite of what you have done. He loves you with a love that will never end and he longs to show you that love.

- He loves you just as much as he loves me and just as much as he loves my brother Soren.

- There is nothing so deep, so dark and so horrible, that he cannot and will not forgive.

And,

- He longs to forgive you for what you have done, Travis.

Here in the quietness of this moment I am offering God's love and forgiveness to you, Travis, and I am also offering you my love and forgiveness.

I will be praying for you and your family that you can accept that love and forgiveness and that someday you can forgive yourself. Love and forgiveness will never change what you have done and what has happened, but a true desire to experience the gift of love and forgiveness that is offered to you can free you from the chains that bind your heart and soul.

If you want some help in understanding just how much God loves you, Travis, ask to see a chaplain in the prison you are placed in. A chaplain will be willing and able to help you. I plead with you to seek that help.

Travis, you have forever impacted our lives in ways that can never be totally understood, but I am now pleading with you and will be praying that you will allow God to make an impact on your life that can affect you for eternity.

As I looked intently into the eyes of my brother's murderer, I felt God's heart beat of forgiveness deep in my own soul. The experience was so deep and rich that it was almost as if my own heart had stopped and God's heartbeat of love, acceptance and forgiveness had permeated and infused every cell of my body. I felt his love pouring over me like soothing, fragrant, warm oil.

As Travis listened to my message his eyes became softer and more intent, then they popped wide open in disbelief, as if to say, "can this possibly be true?' There wasn't a sound in the courtroom. The power of forgiveness touched the hearts of many who witnessed that sacred scene.

Walking back to my seat, I felt a surge of energy I hadn't known for nineteen long months. A heavy burden had been lifted from my shoulders. I had come face to face with my brother's murderer, and I had come face to face with forgiveness.

The message of forgiveness I delivered in the courtroom that day was not based on my own courage or determination. It was straight from the heart of God. I was merely his mouthpiece. At the end of the courtroom proceedings the judge sentenced Travis to life in prison without chance for parole. He was ushered from the room in chains.

It was over.

I learned an important lesson that day. If I had refused to forgive Travis, I would have continued being a victim. I would have been shackled in chains just like Travis, only my chains would have been around my heart and my spirit. I too would have been in prison—the prison of fear, anger and unforgiveness. "When we forgive," Bruce Goettsche once said, "a prisoner is set free, and that prisoner is me."

I left the courthouse a changed woman. I was free.

The media surrounded me with cameras, microphones and recorders. They asked me only one question: "How could you forgive your brother's murderer?"

"I could forgive my brother's murderer because God had drenched me with his love."

Personal Application

WHEN SOMEONE HAS HURT YOU, it is good to identify what that hurt looks like, and how it feels. Describing the outcome of the situation in your life and in your relationships is a valuable exercise. Identifying how the other person's actions have affected you gives voice to your pain, and giving voice to your pain helps in the process of healing.

The best way is to approach this effort in a way that is comfortable and easy for you. You can do this in sentence format, or in point form. It can be short and simple, or it can be more descriptive. It should fit your particular situation, your style and your personality. You can begin your statement by describing how you were hurt—how you were affected physically, emotionally, maritally, socially or financially. One way you can begin is by developing a response to the following statements (or any other statements suited to your situation). These are just a sampling of ways to help you get started in developing your own impact statement.

1. When you said or did (be specific in naming the offense), I felt (choose one or more of the following), or add any number of words or statements that describe your particular experience:

abandoned	exposed	rejected
angry	humiliated	violated
betrayed	hurt	vulnerable
dirty	out of control	

2. As a result of your actions I:

   * can't believe anyone else could like me
   * fear close relationships

- hate myself and who I've become
- no longer trust others
- won't let others close to me

3. When thoughts of you enter my mind, I want to:

- cry
- hide so you'll never find me
- hurt you

- lash out at you
- run away
- scream

Many other thoughts will be triggered by these samples. They are meant only to get you started. Only you know how you were hurt. Make your list as long as you wish—keep going until you have thoroughly exhausted the ways in which you have been affected by the other person. You don't have to develop your statement all at one time. You may want to create it thoughtfully, over a period of time. The important thing is to do it in a way that suits you.

Deep learning can come from any situation, regardless of the simplicity or gravity of the circumstances. Identifying things you've learned from the hurt can dignify your pain, giving you power over what has happened, helping you take another step in the healing process. Hearing your own voice describing the impact of your situation is also important. Reading your statement aloud helps you stay focused and ensures that you say everything you want to say without becoming sidetracked. It is therapeutic to hear your own voice saying the words out loud.

If you are unable to read your thoughts to the person who hurt you, find someone who is willing to listen. It could be a trusted friend or family member. If trust is an issue, you may want to read your statement out loud in the quietness of your own home, imagining that you are telling it to the person who hurt you. Remember that God hears your every word, and even if no one else is around he is willing to listen to you as you pour out your heart to him.

EXPLORATION

1. Who do you blame for your present situation?

2. Was there malicious intent to hurt you on the part of that person?

3. What have you learned about yourself as a result of this situation?

4. What have you learned about the person who hurt you?

5. What discoveries have you made that have helped you? Is there anything that could benefit you, or benefit others in similar circumstances?

6. What is the worst thing that could happen if you forgive the person who hurt you?

7. What is the best thing that could happen if you forgive that person?

PRAYER

O God:

At times I feel so hurt by what has happened. I feel stuck
in this situation and it is affecting my life and my relationship
with others. I feel bitter and resentful about the situation and
I know at times I am not easy to be around. I don't always feel
I can trust others, and consequently that impacts my relationships.
At times I feel consumed by the feelings I rehearse over and over.
At times I even hurt others when my feelings and outbursts
get hurled at people who have nothing to do with
the pain I am experiencing.

I feel ready to move on in my life, but I need help.
Please remove the burden of the past from me. I really do
want to experience freedom from this situation. Help me be
willing to face the facts of how I've been hurt and to then let
go and forgive so I can move on with happiness, freedom and
peace. May I realize that when I withhold forgiveness I am
actually hurting myself more than I am hurting
the one who has harmed me.

Amen.

CHAPTER: XI

FEAR:
Walking through it step by step

UNDERLYING all of our fears
is a lack of trust in ourselves.

—Susan Jeffers

· ·

THE FREEDOM I FOUND through forgiveness was amazing. Despite the pain, hurt, grief and emptiness, I had let go of my anger toward Travis and his family. But in reflecting back over the notion of forgiving Travis, I had felt great trepidation and even fear. The question began to plague me. Why had I been so afraid to forgive?

The facts surrounding Soren's death could never be changed or improved. The only thing I could change was my own attitude. Was I afraid of Travis? No, he couldn't hurt me.

Was I afraid of what forgiveness would mean?

Forgiveness didn't mean that what Travis had done was okay. Forgiveness didn't mean I was condoning what Travis and his brothers had done. It also didn't mean that I was betraying Soren. I had to ask myself the question, is murder unforgivable? I do not believe it is unforgivable. I believe that murder is a terrible atrocity, that there is never an excuse for taking the life of another person. If murder is unforgivable, I asked myself, why would Jesus ask his Father in Heaven to forgive those who were murdering him as he hung on the cross?

"Father forgive them, they know not what they do." The powerful plea made by Jesus on behalf of those who were taking his life as he hung dying on the cross, is an indisputable example that murder is forgivable.

If murder is forgivable, then I still hadn't answered the question of what I was afraid of. I knew I wasn't afraid of what others might think—and besides, they weren't walking in my shoes.

Perhaps, then, I was afraid of what my family would say. Misunderstandings about forgiveness have torn some families apart, with individual members alienated and ostracized for years afterward. I didn't want that to happen in my family. I must admit I had fears—or at least questions—about what my family would think if I offered forgiveness to Travis. Would they understand? Would they think I was a traitor? Would they think I had betrayed Soren? Would they try to talk me out of it? Would they reject me?

As I pondered these questions, I finally came to the conclusion that I couldn't answer any of them with certainty. My brothers and I have a fabulous relationship, but we were separated by a great geographical and emotional distance. Having dealt with death and dying for most of my professional career, I was aware that the grieving process is personal, that family members grieve in different ways, and at different rates. I knew everyone was deeply hurt by Soren's death, but I didn't know where each family member was in the grieving process.

I felt in my heart that my brothers would allow me freedom of thought and expression, even if they didn't necessarily understand or agree with my way of thinking. As for Starli, Pete and Niki, I had no idea how they would react or respond. I could only pray that our relationship would not be damaged.

After analyzing the risks, and balancing those risks against the undeniable direction of God's leading, I came to an unwavering conclusion. I was prepared to relinquish my family relationships rather than walk away from what I knew was God's will for me. Today, as I remember that struggle and the fears I faced, it still brings tears to my eyes.

A Bible passage that spoke strongly to me, helped me make this important decision. *"Everyone who has given up... brothers or sisters or fathers or mothers for my sake, will receive a hundred times as much and will have eternal life." (Matthew 19:29)*

Please don't think for a minute I was attempting to earn anything by being willing to sacrifice family relationships if that was the outcome, but I did understand the potential gravity of the decision I was making. I also knew that if something happened to those important relationships, I would not simply walk away allowing those relationships to be fractured forever.

Relationships are too important to me. I was confident God would help me find the right time and a means to eventually heal those important relationships.

It was also important to put forgiveness into perspective. My Victim Impact Statement identified the intense pain caused by Soren's death as clearly as possible so that Travis and everyone else would understand that it was not okay that he and his brothers had taken Soren's life.

I had floated a trial balloon with my brother, Chris, just hours before presenting our impact statements. Because we were on a similar spiritual path, I quietly told Chris that I was planning to forgive Travis. His head jerked and his eyes blinked in surprise, but he seemed to understand and didn't try to change my mind.

Continuing to work through my list of fears, I arrived at the last item—me. Was I afraid of me? If so, of what in particular was I afraid?

I was afraid I couldn't do it—that I wouldn't be able to carry out my mission based on a divine command to forgive. I was afraid of seeing Travis for the first time—that I would be so repulsed by the sight of the man who had pumped two bullets into my brother that I wouldn't be able to utter words of forgiveness. I was afraid of the emotions that had coursed through me in the weeks and months after Soren's death. I was afraid of being catapulted right back into the emotional hurricane that had ravaged my ordinarily reasonable self.

When it came to the bottom line, I was afraid of no one but myself. That was a harsh reality—to be afraid of my own weakness, afraid of my emotions, afraid of my inability to follow through. Ultimately, I was afraid that I wouldn't be able to stand up for what I believed was a message from God. I was afraid I wasn't strong enough to do what I knew God wanted me to do. I was afraid my faith wasn't strong enough to carry me down the path of forgiveness.

As I thought about all the things that I was afraid of, my mind was flooded with self-doubt. I doubted my strength. I doubted my resolve, my ability, my reasoning, my courage and even my beliefs. My past came rushing back, reminding me of my failures, of the times I had caved instead of doing what was right.

Then I began to realize that the fears and doubts plaguing me were the result of my focus on me. The enemy had me right where he wanted—stuck in the quicksand of fear and doubt. All the negative questions I was asking myself were eroding my faith.

I began to pray that God would harness my fears and rein them in. I took the focus off me, and concentrated my full attention on the one who had healed me after the car accident, who had forgiven me my past and who had given me strength during my weakest moments. Bible texts flooded into my mind. *"My strength is sufficient in your weakness." (2Corinthians 12:8). "I will uphold you with my victorious right hand." (Isaiah 41:10). "With God all things are possible." (Matthew 19:26).*

As these messages washed away my fears and doubts, I realized that strength and grace were being given to me as gifts to replace the fears and doubts that could so easily have prevented me from completing what God wanted me to do. With that realization, I fell to my knees and gave thanks.

· ·

Personal Application

COWARDS AND HEROES ALIKE HAVE FEARS. You and I are no exception. Things in life will always create fear in the depths of our souls. Those fears can be real or they can be imagined, they can be based on fact or they can be irrational. Those individuals who have a fear of heights frequently say they feel they may be forced to jump off a cliff. That feeling is not based on anything factual unless someone has actually tried to force them to jump. Therefore that fear is irrational. Fears can be depressing, intimidating and even paralyzing if you allow them to get the best of you.

Les Hewitt in *The Power of Focus* says, "Firefighters deal with fear every time they enter a burning building. Just before they go into action they experience it—the uncertainty of not knowing if they'll survive or not. An incredible transformation takes place as soon as they go inside the building. They literally step into the fear, and because they do, the fear disappears."

It isn't wrong to be afraid. What is sad, however, is when your fear prevents you from overcoming the obstacles looming before you. Procrastination can be a great factor in keeping us stuck in fear. As you know, fear is one of the places in which we often get stuck. We circle around and around letting our fearful imaginations trap us into thinking we don't have a way to escape. Putting off taking action can keep you stuck for years.

Just like the firefighters, you can step over your fear by looking your fears in the face and making a decision, a decision to take action. Susan Jeffers says, "One of the biggest fears that keeps us from moving ahead with our lives is our difficulty in making decisions." Conversely, action in the face of fear is very liberating.

Each risk you take, each time you move in spite of your fear, you become more powerful. As your power builds, so does your level of confidence. Stretching beyond your comfort zone will become easier and easier as you take those steps important for your healing. Breaking the fear down into steps can make it less intimidating and easier to manage.

In preparing for my Victim Impact Statement, I had choices all along the way. Did I want to attend? Yes or no? Did I want to speak? Yes or no? Did I need to prepare, or should I speak extemporaneously? Did I want others to know ahead of time what I was going to say? Did I need the support of others emotionally removed from the situation? Did I want to forgive? Yes or no?

Even at the last moment when approaching the witness stand, I had a choice. Ironically, I felt like I was facing a wall of fire as I stepped forward to offer forgiveness. Despite the invisible fire, my decision to take that all-important step was one I will never regret.

There has also been fear in my path as I considered speaking publicly about Soren's death and about forgiveness. Even in finishing this book, I face the fear of whether anyone will want to read it. Putting one's experience, learning and perspectives out there for the world to read and potentially criticize is scary. What if my work is a failure? Despite these fears, I have made the choice to push on. I choose to do this for my own continuing personal process of healing and to help others find freedom and peace as well.

You can only fail if you fail to do what you feel compelled to do. Time and effort is never lost. Effort and forward movement creates growth, confidence and a sense of purpose.

Analyze your fears, one by one. Analysis is a powerful way of facing your fear. It isn't difficult. You don't even have to do it all at once. When you choose to stretch and step outside your comfort zone, your fears can actually become stepping stones to action and forward movement. Just taking one deliberate step after another will lead you down the path to health and healing.

EXPLORATION

1. In facing the hurtful situation, what am I afraid of?

2. What are some options available to me in changing this upsetting experience in my life?

   What is the possible outcome of each option?

3. What are the things I fear as I consider taking steps that will help me move on in my own process of healing?

4. What is the worst thing that could happen if I take the action that is causing me to be fearful?

5. What would I do if the worst thing happened?

PRAYER

O God:

I know I face many fears, not only in this particular situation, but also in other areas of my life. I realize I need strength and courage as I face fearful situations. I don't want to cave in and feel powerless in the situations I face just because they cause me to be afraid. Help me to identify my fears and to face them. I want to be strong and courageous. I want to take the action that will help me rise above fearful situations. Thank you for understanding my fear and for loving me anyway.

Amen.

CHAPTER: XII

HEALING WITH LIFERS:

Unexpected opportunities

GOD can forgive anyone who truly repents—even a murderer.

—Billy Graham

· ·

EVERY DAY I GAVE THANKS TO GOD for his amazing work in transforming my life. The incredible impact forgiveness had on me was astounding. I felt like I had received a heart transplant. I now saw life and people in a new light. I saw everyone as having great value regardless of their circumstances, their background or the pot-holes they found themselves in.

I began to feel compassion and concern for people I didn't ordinarily think about —the homeless, prostitutes, wayward youth and prisoners. I truly felt like a new woman. I knew God was calling me to share his grace and mercy with others. Through the encouragement of the leaders in our local Christian Motorcyclists

Association and prison ministry training, we began finding ways of reaching out to people that brought joy and rich experiences to our lives. Clay and I sought visitation status at a nearby provincial corrections facility, meeting with groups of prisoners. After a few weeks the chaplain at the facility asked why I wanted to be involved in prison ministries.

Recognizing the power and conviction of my experience when I told him the story, and the positive impact we were already having on prisoners, he asked if Clay and I would spend Good Friday with prisoners. We would move from area to area throughout the prison complex, sharing our story. The title of our presentation was posted throughout the facility: "I Forgave My Brother's Murderer—You Too Can Be Forgiven"

What an incredible experience it was to see meeting rooms filled to capacity with convicted criminals weeping and accepting God's love. We couldn't believe how thirsty they were for love, acceptance and forgiveness.

I'll never forget walking down the corridor of the protective custody wing one evening, knowing the men behind the locked doors had committed hideous crimes and were in that unit because they needed protection from other prisoners. Walking the long, narrow corridor with the prison chaplain and two men from our Christian Motorcyclists Association, sensing the pain, oppression and weight of their crimes, I started to sob. I felt small and insignificant. In a few short minutes I would be speaking to these prisoners face to face, addressing them in their isolation, their shame and their woundedness. One of my companions, a fellow Christian motorcyclist, put his arm around my shoulder and said, "Annette, that is exactly why you are here. These men need to hear the message God has given you."

The number of men who chose to attend that meeting was astounding, but even more astonishing was the heartfelt response to my message that God loved them in spite of the horrendous things they had done. When I finished speaking, one by one they came close, some with visible tears and some with quavering voices. On almost all of their faces was a miraculous expression of release. It was as if they'd been freed from the shackles of an internal prison, even though they were all returning to their silent cells of segregation.

Each month we met with two different groups of inmates. We presented thoughts of hope, encouragement and love laced with biblical principles to help them in their life struggles and incarceration. Sensing our sincere interest in their lives, they opened up to us with the difficult stories of their backgrounds of abuse, addictions, abandonment, bullying, brutality, control and other heartbreaking pictures of dysfunction and pain. Their wounded hearts and lives enmeshed in the tragedy of unresolved anger and fear overlaid with the shame of rejection, condemnation and now isolation.

They openly shared their gratitude in knowing we truly cared about them, about their wounds, about their healing and about their future. As Clay and I openly shared the joy we found in our ministry to prisoners, new doors began opening. Our message was not about organized religion. It was about God's unconditional gifts of love, acceptance and forgiveness.

The emotional impact it had on me was profound as I sensed the impact it seemed to be having on offenders deep inside prison walls. It seemed that the more I spoke to prisoners and the more I shared about the impact it was having, the more invitations to speak publicly about my miraculous healing in forgiveness arrived. Numerous and diverse, they came not only from Calgary, where I live, but from across Canada and the United States. Churches, professional organizations, women's groups, special events, colleges and universities wanted to understand more fully the gift of forgiveness.

Clay and I sensed a mysterious passion for the hearts of prisoners being kindled in our hearts. We longed to help them understand God's love and forgiveness, and to help them develop (or re-establish) a relationship with God. We realized that their understanding was crucial in the process of healing their own wounds. If their wounds could begin to heal, perhaps the vicious cycle of crime and incarceration might be curtailed.

It was clear to us that God was creating a path for me to influence the lives of others. It was as if he was creating divine appointments so that I could tell others about the wonder of his love. Taxi drivers, university professors, flight attendants, pilots, doctors, lawyers, FBI agents and auditoriums filled with people heard the truth about God's love and forgiveness.

I knew that only God could orchestrate what was happening. It was his love and his forgiveness touching the hearts of these people. God has ways and means far beyond our ability to dream, or even to imagine. Just when I think I have life figured out, something new, exciting and totally unexpected comes along.

After attending a restorative justice meeting, the director of Community Justice Ministries invited me to sit on a Life-Line Management Board that provided support for federal prison In-Reach Workers who assist lifers—men and women serving life sentences for crimes of violence. Offered through the Mennonite Church, the Life-Line service included volunteers from many denominations. That I was a family member of a homicide victim, along with my executive abilities, had sparked their interest. They wanted me to bring the perspective of a surviving family member to the board. I agreed to observe at least one meeting to see if this would be a good fit.

At the end of the meeting I was invited to share a brief synopsis of my leadership background and my personal experience. I told them about Soren's death and the journey of healing that had led me to forgive my brother's murderer in the courtroom, and how that act of forgiveness had changed me so dramatically. I also spoke of my emerging passion for helping prisoners understand how much God loves them in spite of what they've done.

As I spoke, I sensed deep feeling in the room. Three men stood and with gripping emotion expressed regret for the death of my brother. Then they each revealed that they had taken the life of another human being! These men had incredible stories. They were so well-spoken, yet each had been convicted of murder. Having done their time in prison, they were now living life sentences on parole as upstanding, productive, trustworthy men —men who would forever carry the scars of an impetuous act.

Each of the men cautiously and gently approached me, and we embraced in a hug with humility, tears and amazement. Who would have dreamed that one day I would hug three men convicted of murder? That interaction created another healing miracle that I will never forget.

Unquestionably, I felt that a role on the Life-Line Management Board would provide me with an opportunity to help lifers serving time in federal prison. In addition, it might also aid in my own ongoing quest for healing. On the spot I agreed to join, and after a few months on the board I was asked if I would feel comfortable conducting a three-hour evening workshop for a group of lifers. After careful thought and prayer I agreed, with the provision that my husband also participate.

Up until then we had been working with short-term offenders. We had always found the inmates to be respectful and happy that someone was concerned about them and willing to spend time with them. Safety was never a concern.

In restorative justice circles, hearing from a victim and the victim's family is an important aspect of the inmate's healing process. Sharing that story is equally healing for the victim. As we planned the session, we prayed that God would prepare the way, and that he would open the hearts of the embittered and no doubt calloused men we would be meeting with.

In my own heart, I vacillated about whether I was ready for an encounter with a roomful of people who had taken the life of another human being. Anxiety and fear were again trying to control me, but this time prayer calmed my vulnerability and reduced my temptation to run away from the experience. I knew I didn't owe the inmates anything. I realized we had some experience and information to share with them that they might not hear in any other way. We actually owed that to God, not to these lifers.

Little did I know that they, too, were afraid of what they would hear. I also had no idea they had something to give me—something I could receive in no other way.

When we entered the room, we were amazed that it was filled to capacity. Inmates from three different federal prisons, all serving life sentences, along with some who were out on parole, were in attendance along with a number of support workers including corrections officers, a psychologist, a social worker, two Life -Line In-Reach Workers, two prison chaplains and the director of Community Justice Ministries.

When I stood to speak I looked around the room, overwhelmed by the enormously excruciating pain that these inmates and parolees had created in the lives, families and communities of their victims, and in their own families and communities. I opened my mouth, but not a sound came out. I stood there speechless, with every eye riveted on me.

Looking around the room, I suddenly realized that God loved every person I locked eyes with regardless of their crime. What a moment of grace! What a revelation! When I acknowledged in my heart that God loved these people, I was finally able to speak. "Be honest with these men," I heard God saying as I spoke. I knew

God was pushing me to share something I had never shared with another human being. It was difficult to be so vulnerable, but I finally confessed that early in the aftermath of Soren's death I was so distraught, so full of rage that had the circumstances been right I could have killed my brother's murderer.

My confession placed me on level ground with the lifers. I realized at that moment how easily rage, selfishness, fear and pent-up emotion can cause devastating actions. Along with our story of forgiveness, we offered God's love and forgiveness to every person in the room. Clay sang the heart-gripping songs *In Heaven's Eyes* and *His Eyes of Mercy*, and together we prayed. Needless to say they were amazed and moved by what they had just seen, heard and experienced.

During the incredibly open and meaningful facilitated discussion that followed, we developed a mind-boggling list of the impacts of their offenses. In a moment of self-awareness, one inmate burst out, "Who haven't we impacted?" By the end of the evening the men were openly sharing deep remorse, regret and shame for what they had done. Those men were repenting that night, and I believe God was forgiving them.

Some had been in prison for more than twenty years but had never had an opportunity to explore how their actions had affected their own families and communities or the families of their victims.

One by one they opened up. Listening to them speak, Clay and I experienced no shock, judgment or criticism, in spite of what they were telling us. God had given us the ability to see beyond the things they had done. We saw them as men precious in his sight. Even though they had done terrible things, it was obvious they were not necessarily terrible people.

I can't begin to describe the healing that happened for me, too, as I heard the shame and sadness in their comments. It gave me hope to know these men were so full of remorse.

We openly shared each other's pain—me the pain of Soren's death; they the pain of shame. We were turning to each other in our tears, and regret. Together we were healing.

As we drove home that night I felt as if I had just received another huge gift—this one from the most unlikely of places. My latest gift of healing had come from a roomful of individuals serving life sentences for murder!

Personal Application

ALLOWING GOD TO LEAD THE WAY to your healing is an important principle. When opportunities arise, you can easily slam the door, saying, "I don't want any part of this. It's too scary. It's not what I signed up for. Furthermore, what's the point?"

The mere thought of contact with the person causing your pain can be terrifying. It may be mind-boggling to even imagine being with the person you despise, whether that individual has intentionally or unintentionally hurt you.

If you truly want healing in your life, you have to be willing to face your fears. You need to be open to healing in whatever form it might come. You need to be willing to stretch beyond your zone of comfort. You need to make choices that take you beyond being stuck, beyond the places that keep you mired in the mud of your own anger, blame and fear.

You may be surprised by the outcome. The rewards inherent in taking courageous steps, and in stretching beyond what you've done before can be phenomenal. If God gives you something to do, or shows you the way he wants you to go, he will also enable you.

EXPLORATION

1. Who do you need to talk with, write to or interact with in some way?

2. Why should you connect with that person?

3. What will you say?

4. What is holding you back?

5. What is the outcome you are hoping for?

6. What type of help or support do you need?

7. What if the other person does not respond in the way you are hoping for?

PRAYER

O God:

The healing journey isn't easy. I want so much to find answers, and I long to understand why that person hurt me. I really need to know how the person feels about what he/she did and even why it happened. I need to know what to do next and how to do it. I know my fear, anxiety and the grudge I carry is heavy, and it is holding me back from having a full and happy life. I sometimes even feel paralyzed in being able to do anything about the situation. Please create a path that will help me, but please make it something I can handle with your help.

Amen.

CHAPTER: XIII

BITTERNESS:
Releasing the past

THINGS we do not face will continue
to create pain. We must name them, identify
how they hurt, and let them go.

—Annette Stanwick

....

THOSE OF US ON THE OUTSIDE can't begin to imagine what
it is like to spend fifteen, twenty or thirty years in prison.
The minute an inmate enters prison, the world stops. Picture
yourself locked away from society, locked away from the growth
and progress of the world.

Totally isolated from life on the outside, inmates follow the
same rigid routine day after day, month after month, year after
year. Time for them stands still. Life enters a time warp consisting
of checks, cell counts, searches, iron gates slamming shut, mundane institutional meals, lock-downs and an almost complete lack
of stimulation that those of us on the outside experience on a
daily basis. With the exception of prescribed programs, books and

newspapers, their growth and improvement is minimal unless they are personally motivated to learn and improve themselves within the prison setting. The only personal contact they have with the outside world is the daily contact with prison workers and occasional visits from a chaplain, volunteer or family member.

Clay and I began meeting with groups of lifers on a monthly basis. Before and after our presentations we always mingled with the men and women in a group. Where time and opportunity allowed, we also talked quietly one on one, establishing more and more trust. We encouraged them to use their time of incarceration and parole profitably through reading, study, personal reflection and spiritual development.

As we met with lifers, I became increasingly interested in the restorative justice movement. This movement is based on the premise that people doing time are real individuals with real hearts and lives who have made poor choices. Criminal justice demands that they serve prison time, but restorative justice exerts that we can help restore these individuals. We can help them deal with their past and restore their dignity and self-esteem in spite of their incarceration.

While the criminal justice system is based on retribution for the crimes committed, the restorative system is based on redeeming the individual. Restorative measures can help them come to grips with what they have done. These measures can help inmates face their past yet develop healthy and whole lifestyles, whether they remain inside prison walls or are released into society.

Prior to becoming involved with inmates, I was a motivational speaker. Over the years my passion to inspire and motivate people had helped many find happiness and joy in their lives. A large percentage of my speaking was of a spiritual nature. I found incredible gratification in seeing the lights come on in people's eyes when they realized they were of tremendous value to God.

Clay and I soon realized that much of the material I had presented over the years in my speaking engagements across North America could be adapted for restorative justice purposes. Clay's background as a pastor would help enrich our presentations. Added to this formula was the fact that we had always enjoyed co-presenting at events. It was as though our years of experience had been grooming us for this new prison setting.

We developed a five-part series called the *IOU Seminars— Inward, Outward and Upward: a Journey Toward Healing.* Under the wings of the Life-Line project and with assistance from one of the in-reach workers, we proposed those seminars to the wardens at two federal prisons in Alberta.

One warden responded with tears in his eyes. "Lifers are the forgotten of society," he said. Both wardens were incredibly supportive. They could hardly imagine that a family member of a victim of homicide would have a desire to reach out to these men. Encouraging us to move forward, they offered to arrange for staff to facilitate our visits for weekend seminars.

The seminars went very well. Each session brought new and rich experiences. We attempted to motivate the lifers to look deep in their own hearts and lives, to reach new levels of belief in themselves and in a God who loved them outrageously.

One memorable weekend, Clay and I were in the midst of a session entitled, "The Mystery and Miracle of Forgiveness." We were focusing on how resentment and bitterness can become toxic when we hold on to past hurts and offenses.

As we store up the list of real and imagined injuries that we've suffered at the hands of others, the toxicity builds. With the slightest provocation the injury can reappear, and once again we rehearse and relive the hurt. The poison of pain builds up inside us like a head of steam, ready to explode. We become like boilers with no release valve.

As we talked, I decided to do something I had never done before. Though I loved my mother deeply, she had a personality type that harbored a deep level of anger and resentment throughout her entire life. With the slightest provocation, she'd pull out her "Bitterness List."

I began to share my mother's story with these lifers. I had heard my mother's list of annoyances, hurts and perceived offenses recounted hundreds of times over the years. I honestly didn't know how to help her. "Mom you need to let that go," I would tell her. "You are only hurting yourself by reliving all this stuff that happened so long ago. I am not denying that it happened, and I am not saying it didn't hurt at the time, but you can't change the past. You need to let go and move on."

Unfortunately, neither I nor any of the professionals we hired could help my mother. In later years she became bitter, angry and lonely. She needed people desperately, but in her bitterness she destroyed relationships. In her anger she pushed people away and in her mistrust she grew lonelier with each passing year. She didn't understand that her anger hurt her more than it hurt the person she was angry with, or that her bitterness caused her more harm than it caused the person she resented.

When we store up misdemeanors and bitterness, regardless of their origin or severity, our pent-up emotions can become toxic. We can become suspicious and paranoid in our relationships with others. That suspicion and paranoia can create a distorted picture of reality, often manifesting itself in an irrational fear of what we think others are thinking, doing or saying about us.

I compared our list of hurts to that of a snowball pushed off a mountain top. As the snowball rolls it gathers more snow, becoming larger and larger, rolling faster and faster, gaining momentum, power and weight until it finally crashes like an avalanche into something at the bottom and explodes with great force. As it rolls,

I said, the snowball destroys everything in its path, and at the end it lays there in a crumpled, broken heap. As I spoke these words, carefully watching the non-verbal response of the men in front of me, men whose own lives had erupted in uncontrolled behavior resulting in the death of another human being, I noticed one individual in particular. With a reddened face and eyes brimming with tears, he was unable to restrain himself. "If only someone had told me about anger and resentment as a young boy," he finally burst forth, "maybe I wouldn't have killed four members of my very own family!"

The room fell into a stunned silence. With careful encouragement, he described how he still carried a bitterness list of resentments he had harbored from a very young age. With gentle probing, he admitted that many of the things on his list were small and insignificant. Nevertheless, over time the pressure caused by the increasing number of things on his list had mounted, and one day he couldn't stand it anymore. He exploded in a white-hot rage that destroyed the lives of those he loved.

At the time of his violently explosive behavior, he recounted, he wasn't even aware of the potential consequences. He just needed to stop the hurting deep inside him, and his tragic actions made it stop. Some weeks later an individual close to this prisoner confided that after our session regarding bitterness and forgiveness he had actually accepted God's love and forgiveness in the privacy of his own cell. He had also said that he knew he would never have the right to happiness, but in spite of that he truly felt forgiven by God.

April 16, 2007, as this book was in its final stages, the media was ablaze with the stories of the Virginia Massacre at Virginia Tech. Cho Seung-Hui gunned down thirty-two students and faculty.

The interviews along with the videos and statements made by the assassin himself painted stunning pictures of a young man who was lonely, rejected, wounded and irrepressibly angry. His bitterness was unbelievably deep and seething. In seemingly hopeless desperation in trying to stop the pain, he exploded in a volcanic rage that destroyed thirty-two lives. His rage then turned inward on himself. His pain and anger ended along with his life. If only he'd been shown how to deal with his bitterness and wounds, the lives of thirty-three precious people could have been spared, including his own.

. . . .

PERSONAL APPLICATION

YOUR PAIN AND RESENTMENT ARE TOXIC. You must deal with the bitterness. Releasing pain requires courage, but it is necessary if you are to move forward. One of the most important aspects of healing your past is letting go of it. It can actually be a visual, auditory or even a physical experience.

Hold your hands in front of you, clenching your fists tightly. Hold onto the offense that is creating your pain. Imagine that the hurt you're holding in your fists is a burning ember. You want to hurl it at the persons who hurt you, but you want to wait until it will do the most damage. Perhaps you need to build enough courage to hurl it. In the meantime, the ember is burning a hole in your own flesh.

Say to yourself, "I don't want to be hurt by this thing anymore. I don't want to continue to experience this pain, or to harbor these feelings. They are not hurting the person who hurt me. They are only hurting me, making me more bitter, resentful, mistrusting and hateful. I want to let go and get on with my life, and I want the hurting to end. I cannot change what happened in the past. I want to change my life now, and I want to be more positive in the future."

Now open your fists and let go of that burning ember. Imagine it dropping to the ground. Visually and physically walk away from the smoldering ember. Cover it with dirt if you want. You can even dig an imaginary hole and bury it until it smothers and dies. You can crush it with heavy boots, or you can dowse it with a pail of water or throw it into the deepest ocean. Do whatever works.

....

EXPLORATION

1. What resentments are you harboring that continue to surface time and time again?

2. Who is being hurt by the bitterness and resentment you are holding inside?

3. When has your pent-up anger surfaced or exploded unexpectedly?

4. How did your bitter outburst affect the target of your pent-up emotions?

5. How were you affected by what happened as a result of your actions or words?

PRAYER

O God:

I long to be free of my resentments. I know I've carried
resentment and anger around like a heavy burden. I've picked at
my old wounds for so long; yet others are as fresh as this week.
I realize the pattern of holding on to the past hurts me. I know
that holding on is not helpful to me or to my happiness, my peace
of mind and my relationship with others. Please help me identify
those things that create barriers in my relationships. As I face
the memories and situations that I'm hanging on to—memories
that are hurting no one but me—give me the wisdom, the
strength and even the willingness to release them.
Please help me accept that it is in letting go
that I will find healing.

Amen.

CHAPTER: XIV

A TRUE ARTIST:
The strength and beauty of scars

GOD wants to transform every
form of human suffering into
something glorious.

—Elisabeth Elliott

• •

OUR FRIEND CARL BELYEA, an artist whose creativity
we find full of beauty and meaning, sculpted a dignified
African-American man out of Manitoba maple. The first time
I saw the magnificent sculpture in Carl's home, I felt a strong
emotional connection. I felt compelled to reach out and caress the
satiny smoothness of the perfectly shaped head. Gazing into
the eyes of Carl's make-believe man, I wondered what experiences
in his life had turned him into a piece of art.

I also have an artist hiding inside me. I love beautiful things and
have a passion for color, texture and creativity. I enjoy designing
beautiful vignettes in our home and in our yard, and I gain
great satisfaction in creating meaningful symbolic visual displays

to enhance our church worship services. In keeping with my interest in artistry, and in preparation for one of my presentations entitled "The Artistry of God," I called Carl and asked to visit his art studio. I asked him to assist me in understanding the mind and processes of an artist. He graciously assented to my visit.

In his studio Carl showed me raw materials awaiting his artistic touch, along with diagrams of works he dreamed of creating. He showed me pieces that were in progress, and work that was nearly finished. His studio was filled with stained glass pieces, metal sculptures, rock formations, fountains and woodcarvings. Stacks of gnarled, bark-covered tree trunks and branches that looked ready for a bonfire were actually pieces Carl envisioned developing into artistic creations. He recognized beauty deep inside those hunks of wood, and saw how one day they could emerge into stunning sculptures.

Then I saw the magnificent woodcarving of the African-American man that I had seen earlier on display in his home. I went to the piece and stood again in wonder, stroking the beautiful work of art. To my astonishment, my fingers felt a deep crack extending from behind his ear to the base. Running my fingers over his head and down his strong neck, I was stunned. Looking closer, I saw another crack down the front.

"Carl, what happened?" I cried, thinking that the beautiful piece was wounded and spoiled. Carl explained the risk of woodcarving. Climate affects wood, and the sculptor can never be assured that the wood is dry enough not to crack.

"What will you do with this piece?" I asked. In my imagination, the work was ruined. Maybe it would sit on a shelf forever cracked; or perhaps it would eventually be chopped into smaller chunks and recycled into smaller carvings.

"Annette," he said, taking a deep breath to overcome his grief at the cracks in the masterpiece he had spent hours perfecting.

"I will do whatever it takes. I have to be sure the cracking is finished, and then I will clean it out thoroughly, ensuring that all the splinters and bits of debris are removed. I'll fill the cracks with solder and fine sawdust made from the same Manitoba maple, and I'll mix that in with some special glue."

"I will do whatever it takes." To me, that was Carl's most telling statement. He wasn't prepared to let go of the wonderful piece he had created. That, I thought, is how God is with us. God grieves when we are wounded, and when we stray from his side. He doesn't want to let us go, and he'll do whatever it takes to restore us. *"We are his workmanship." (Ephesians 2:10).* In Greek this means "We are his work of art."

Later that year we attended Carl's art show. Once again I found myself in awe of his creations. Each piece was unique and well done. To my amazement, he had even created stained glass motorcycle replicas that were absolutely awesome.

On display in a place of honor I saw the magnificent bust of the African–American man. Gazing at its wonderful expression of strength and pride, I was afraid to place my hand on it. I finally reached out and touched his head, searching inquisitively for evidence of the cracks that had once marred its beauty. Instead of gaping wounds, I found added texture, grain, and color that now made the carving even more striking and interesting.

A true artist, Carl had created this piece and was grieved by its gaping wounds, yet he wasn't willing to place it on the shelf termed useless. Nor was he willing to discard it, or destroy it. He loved that piece of art because he had invested so much of himself in it, and he had found a way to restore his precious creation.

Carl's perseverance is incredibly symbolic of the work God is willing to do in our lives. Just like Carl, God is loving and creative, and he is able to find ways to restore us when we're broken. Divorce, criticism, betrayal, relationship meltdown and other hurtful happenings leave deep scars that need to be addressed. It is important to remember that healing doesn't happen overnight. Because of the climate we grew up in coupled with our own weaknesses and fears, healing may take time and careful patient work. We need to address one layer at a time, perhaps over and over, before the wound is finally cleaned of the debris left over from painful experiences.

This process of debriding and digging out the wound might be painful. As God removes the ungodly characteristics, the cracks may need to ooze and weep for some time before the restoration can actually begin.

I love those scars on Carl's creation. I'm sure that he worked to restore his masterpiece with gentle care so as not to extend the crack or create an even deeper wound. I'm sure he worked thoughtfully, pondering each step, each process and each move to ensure that the beauty of his work would be preserved. The original carving could only rest and submit to his creative process; the piece of art could not restore itself.

Looking at Carl's sculpture, I realized that we cannot heal ourselves. We cannot restore our own emotional stability. We cannot even recover our own strength, because we don't know the processes that need to occur. What we need to do is simply submit to the tender touch of the master designer, allowing him to work within us, to restore us into the person he wants us to become. All we can do is place ourselves in his workshop by surrendering to him. The psalmist David said, *I cried out to you and you healed me. (Psalm 30:2)* Just as Carl mended the cracks in his beautiful carving, God is able to heal our wounds if we cry out to him. Sensing the significance of his scarred sculpture, Carl has named the piece "David".

Carl was unable to remove the scars on his statue. He chose to work with the wounds rather than to disguise them in some unnatural way. It is the same with us. While our physical wounds are usually visible, our emotional scars are usually out of sight. Scars themselves are not normally painful. It is the process of wounding that creates the pain. Scars, however, are constant reminders that we have suffered an insult.

I love the title of Sharon Jaynes book, *Your Scars are Beautiful to God*. In essence, she is saying that our scars and our stories of healing are evidence that God has been working in our lives.

Pondering that thought, I think of the physical scars I carry from our accident, but I also imagine the scar on my heart regarding Soren's death. I know I will forever be grateful for the healing miracles of love and forgiveness that turned my painful wounds into something significant that God could use.

. . . .

PERSONAL APPLICATION

YOU MAY HAVE WOUNDS OR MEMORIES that have created deep scars. They may cause you continuing pain and sorrow. The actions or neglect you have experienced may have left you broken and longing for love. You may feel that your past has made you useless, tarnished, unloved or even unlovable.

In the case of the inmate and the Virginia Massacre mentioned in the previous chapter, their wounds had not had the opportunity to crack open, ooze and weep. The painful bitterness that had collected deep in their wounded souls were left gaping open, unattended and perhaps even denied by those closest to them.

It is important to realize that regardless of what has happened in your life, God loves you no matter how deep or how horrid your wound. To be healed, you must first acknowledge that you have been hurt, and then you need to be willing to allow God to do his work. Being willing to allow God so close in your life can be scary and threatening, especially if your wounds came from someone you should have been able to trust. The person who violated, abused, or neglected you may not be trustworthy, but God can always be trusted. He has your best interest at heart.

Often the painful past is so familiar that you do not want to let go of it. Life without the familiar, as bad as the familiar was, is a fearful place. The important thing is to tell God about your wound. It isn't complicated. Talk about your wound, telling him where it hurts and how it feels. He can even help you find someone to help heal your wounds. He can work through others to bring healing to you.

Examining the wounds, understanding what happened and how it hurts along with letting go of the stuff in the past is like removing the debris. Healing the wound doesn't erase the memory, but it can make the memory less painful. It can bring a different perspective to the situation. It can help you resume life in a more meaningful and peaceful fashion. Ask God to heal you and to restore you. He delights in bringing you back to wholeness. All you have to do is allow him to work in your life. Just as an artist can create something beautiful from a piece of wood, so can God's love create something meaningful from your life. You are his living masterpiece.

. . . .

EXPLORATION

1. What events or times have created your deepest wounds?

2. How do those events continue to bother you or prevent you from being all that you are meant to be?

3. What memories and scars in your life continue to find their way into your thoughts?

4. What scars continue to interfere in your relationships?

5. When you think of being healed and restored, what do you hope for?

PRAYER

O God:

Right now I long to be whole and happy. I lay open my
bruised and wounded heart for you to see. I realize it is
impossible for me to heal these things on my own. I realize
I am in deep need, and I believe you can help me in ways I never
thought possible. I know I am afraid at times, because I don't know
what the future will bring if I am healed, but I want to trust and
I want to be whole. I long for my life and circumstances to change.
I need to find release from the hurtful situations I continue to hang
onto. I also long for my life to be meaningful. I need your power
in my life to set me free from the scars that are constricting,
sometimes holding me tight in their clutches. I ask you to
bring something good and meaningful out of my painful
experiences. Thank you for your unending patience
with me. Thank you for your love and the creativity
that you are willing to use in my life.

Amen.

CHAPTER: XV

THE MYSTERY AND MIRACLE:
Understanding forgiveness

FORGIVENESS helps us empty the recycle bin of our hearts.

—Ryan Walter

● ●

WE LIVE IN A WORLD of shattered relationships. Every day in our homes, schools and churches; in our families and communities; in the places where we work and play, relationships are broken. People in broken relationships avoid each other. When contact is unavoidable there may be pleasant smiles and polite gestures, but that is as deep as it goes. Superficiality is not meaningful connection.

At some point in our lives we all have been hurt, and we have hurt others. Everywhere we go, all over the world, people hurt each other. Wounded people are everywhere. Painful as it is to live in this world of shattered relationships and wounded people, there is no alternative. Until we deal with the wounds in our lives, shattered and broken relationships will continue. Unless we find a way of dealing with the pain, the hurt will continue for the rest of our lives. The chasm that occurs with broken relationships spreads into other relationships, eventually influencing our children's ability to deal with painful situations, creating a ripple effect like a pebble dropped in a pond.

I believe the solution is forgiveness. Forgiveness is about healing wounds and relationships. Forgiveness is God's remarkable plan for healing wounds. We were not created to hurt other people, and we were not created to heal those hurts. That is why God developed his plan for forgiveness—to restore broken relationships. The most important relationship that needs restoring is your relationship with God. He created forgiveness to make reconciliation with him possible. Through forgiveness, our other relationship wounds are also healed.

Much mystery surrounds the notion of forgiveness. What is forgiveness? What is it not? Why do we need it? How does forgiveness work? Why should we forgive, and how in the world can we forgive? Some things we will perhaps never truly understand, but it is important to unravel some of the mystery inherent in those questions. When we forgive others, we open ourselves up to being misunderstood, but we also open ourselves to tremendous hidden gifts and blessings. Through those blessings we are given the ability to make positive choices, and we receive the power to resist and overcome bitterness. When something hurtful happens, the need for revenge is strong. But lashing out, hurting, demeaning, punishing or even slaying the person responsible for the hurt doesn't heal the wound.

If reconciliation is to occur, both parties must be willing. I experienced the miracle of reconciliation through forgiveness decades ago when I shamefully stepped outside our marriage for a time. Despite being deeply hurt by my terrible actions, my husband chose to forgive me. In that act of forgiveness, he chose to look beyond what I had done. He shifted his focus to what our relationship could become if we both worked at healing the fracture I had caused. Since then we have both worked hard in healing our marriage, and we continue to be grateful for the wonderful closeness we have today. His love and forgiveness affected me in ways I can never begin to explain. I will love him forever for the grace and mercy he showed to me.

In that situation I also experienced God's unconditional love and forgiveness. Through God's gift of forgiveness I experienced complete victory and freedom from my past mistake. That whole scenario serves as yet another anchor for me in my healing journey. I am very aware that other marriages may not be reconciled in the same way. Some partners in a marriage may have layers and layers of pain to deal with, pain that takes many years to heal. Others may have irreconcilable differences that prevent them from finding peace and harmony in that relationship.

Regardless of whether it is a marriage that is in need of reconciliation or a relationship with a family member or a friend or business associate, forgiveness is an essential part of healing. We need to heal the wound to become unstuck. However, forgiveness is a complex process often requiring ongoing decisions, multiple choices and abundant courage.

Our willingness to do the work in order to heal the hurts we've experienced is paramount if we are to find peace, power and even purpose in our present circumstances. Doing the work can ultimately help us find a way for joy and happiness in our life. We are each responsible our own growth regardless of the circumstances.

When we are willing to forgive, we may receive courage beyond our normal abilities. I know I was given an extraordinary measure of courage and strength that day in the courtroom when I forgave Travis. Fear and pride are strong forces that may prevent us from letting go of the hurt, but when we forgive we trade our pride for the gift of peace. Forgiveness and peace both come straight from the heart of God. Please don't allow fear and pride to keep you from experiencing healing in your life.

Compassion is another important step in the healing process. When God taught me that my brother's murderer was deeply wounded, I had no idea how that thought would initiate a sense of compassion for his whole family, but eventually I came to see how the circumstances of their lives had contributed to their terrible choices. In the book *Social Intelligence,* author Daniel Goleman says, "Hatred spreads all the more readily when individuals have been victimized in the past, and they still feel wounded or wronged. When tensions rise, they feel a need to resort to violence to defend themselves, even when their self-defense results in… murder. "

Never could the background of that family excuse what they had done, but I truly began to see them them through eyes of compassion rather than eyes filled with hatred. When we forgive, we begin to see the person who caused the harm as someone with great needs and hurts, as someone stuck in a world of anger and fear.

Forgiveness does not mean that we are required to trust the offender. Our forgiveness does not and cannot condone the offender's behavior. Our forgiveness cannot even ensure that the offender will accept our forgiveness. Nor can forgiveness ensure that the offender will be repentant or remorseful.

Even though Travis had confessed, he had not apologized or repented, and he had not asked for forgiveness. My forgiveness of Travis was not based on anything he had done. My forgiveness came from God prompting me to forgive.

I love the statement by Ryan Walter, a well-known hockey player, who said that "forgiveness helps us empty the recycle bin of our hearts." In our woundedness, it is so easy to recycle the hurts, misdemeanors and accusations over and over. But through forgiveness we can get rid of them forever. Forgiveness helps us put our past in the past. It helps us begin to rebuild our lives.

Because forgiveness changes people, scientists have been curious about the mystery that surrounds it. There is scientific evidence that forgiveness actually changes us at the cellular level. Dr. Fred Luskin, now deceased, was director and co-founder of the Stanford University Forgiveness Project. That groundbreaking study provided new insights into the healing powers and medical benefits of forgiveness.

Goleman references that study. He states, "Holding onto hatred and grudges has grave physiological consequence. Studies reveal that every time people think of those they hate, their own body responds with pent-up anger; it floods their system with stress hormones, raises their blood pressure and even impairs their immune system. Taking that a step further, the more frequently and intensely their muted rage is repeated, the more risk there is of lasting biological consequence."

Goleman goes on to say that, conversely, "Forgiving someone we carry a grudge against reverses the biological reaction; it lowers our blood pressure, heart rate, and levels of stress hormones and it lessens our pain and depression."

The only alternative to forgiveness is unforgiveness, and unforgiveness is like a cancer. It eats away at you inside, keeping you imprisoned in your resentments, bitterness and hatred. Unforgiveness keeps you handcuffed to the hate and blame, month after month and year after year. Unforgiveness keeps you stuck in a negative rut. Remaining stuck not only punishes you, it punishes your family and those around you as you become consumed by criticism and fault-finding and the ever-deepening chasm of unresolved issues.

On the farm and ranch where I was raised I remember many instances of being stuck, either in deep snowdrifts or in the mud after the snow melted or after a heavy rain. No matter how much we raced the motor and spun the wheels, just sitting there never got us unstuck. We had to do something. If we did nothing, we didn't move. We had to dig ourselves out, or push with all our might, or get another vehicle to pull us out.

It's the same in our lives. If we are stuck spinning our wheels in a wounded relationship, we are at an impasse. We can't move on to a place of freedom and peace unless we forgive. It doesn't matter who hurt who first. Someone needs to build a bridge, and that someone is you!

Holding onto unforgiveness is a major factor in remaining stuck. Lance Morrow said, "To not forgive is to be imprisoned by the past, by old grievances that do not permit life to proceed with new business. To not forgive is to yield oneself to another's control… to be locked into a sequence of act and response, of outrage and revenge, tit for tat, escalating always. The present is endlessly overwhelmed and devoured by the past. Forgiveness frees the forgiver. It extracts the forgiver from someone else's nightmare."

If we don't find a way to deal with the hurts, one connection after another will end in the trash can of discarded relationships. Life becomes isolated and lonely when there is no healing and no release from the weight of grudges. The load can become unbearable. Sadness, emptiness, depression, paranoia and even hopelessness set in. Another important point to remember is that when we forgive, we do not place our well-being in the hands of the one who harmed us. William Ward said, "Forgiveness is the key that unlocks the handcuffs of hate." Forgiveness enables us to enter into the painful experience without the horrible hatefulness that once may have consumed our thinking, making us feel bitter and even vengeful.

In the end, when we forgive we are still wounded, but our woundedness is no longer a consuming force. We may still have a deep ache, but that ache is transformed into an ability to lay aside the pain, to rise up and move on. Forgiveness brings peace. It frees us to be lifted above our past and our present, and to begin living our future in a new way.

One day as I was bringing this book to its final stages, I had an encounter that was not coincidental. Interviewing a doctor for a fellowship position, I asked her, "What is the most difficult experience you have had, and how did you handle it?"

"The murder of my brother was my most difficult experience," the doctor replied. "In handling it, I forgave the person who took his life." I was shocked, and when the doctor learned I was writing a book about my own similar life-altering experience, we were both amazed. "Tell your readers that forgiveness is the best thing you can do for yourself," she said.

When you forgive, bitterness is replaced by a sense of freedom and peace. Freedom may come with an overwhelming sense of gratitude—at last you have found comfort and release. Forgiveness may eventually bring something new and meaningful into your life. You may not be able to describe what has happened, but you will be able to see and feel the results. That is part of the mystery and miracle of forgiveness.

I know that God performed a miracle in me. I saw and felt the miracle. When I released my heart into God's hands and allowed him to work his miracle of forgiveness, I experienced a transformation. When I forgave as he told me to, he healed me and set me free.

It wasn't easy, and from time to time I continue to be afraid. When I doubt myself, the enemy within quickly begins hurling sharp arrows of self-sabotage. "Who do you think you are, writing a book on forgiveness? You're not an expert on relationships!"

he sneers. "Who would want to read your thoughts, or listen to you speak?" Those are just a few of the prickly notions I battle from time to time.

Despite my fears, God's healing mercy has moved me from a role of victim to a role of victor. He took me from a position of powerlessness to a place of new strength. Instead of continually walking in a nightmare, I began to walk in a place of peace and purpose. I went from feeling out of control to being able to manage my actions, thoughts and emotions. My weakness, depression and grief was replaced with strength, courage and energy. I began focusing on others instead of "poor me." I went from weeping at the hideousness life had handed me to feeling a pure sense of joy at the vision God had created for my life.

Part of that vision is to share what God has done hoping you might also find a way through your painful place. Maya Angelou said, "When you learn, teach. When you get, give." I have learned much through this experience—more than I can possibly put into this book. I have received so many wonderful blessings that I want to give back to the God who has given me so much. As a result of my transformation, I feel compelled to bring hope to others.

As we shared our thoughts and experiences of forgiving the person who had taken the life of someone so close to our hearts, we both realized that we had released our hold on the bitterness, anger, hatred and resentment that was hurting no one but ourselves. Releasing those toxic emotions was inherent in the "letting go" phase of the healing process. The act of releasing and letting go enabled us to move to the pivotal point of forgiveness.

Hearts and homes everywhere have been touched or challenged by hurtful situations. You are no exception. You deserve to be free from the internal prison that is created by hanging on to hurts.

Forgiveness is a pathway of hope that will help you on your journey of healing. May your life and heart be transformed as you travel your own path paved with positive choices. May the mystery and miracle of forgiveness transform you and set you free. When you find freedom you will also find peace.

How can forgiveness make such a difference? That is the mystery and the miracle.

PERSONAL APPLICATION

YOU MAY BE SAYING, "I'm not sure forgiveness is for me. It's a tall order, and I'm not sure I can do it. Maybe it would be easier to stay where I am, rather than trying to change when I don't even know how."

Rest assured that it isn't easy, especially when you rely only on your own strength. Better to let go and let God handle the situation. He knows the way. He can make the path straight and he will enable you in ways you never thought possible.

You may be asking, "What if, when I offer forgiveness, the person who hurt me doesn't respond in a way I would like?"

Good question. What that person does with your offer of forgiveness is not your responsibility. You can only be responsible for your own actions. Forgiveness is actually about you, and for you. It is about letting go of pain, hurt, bitterness and hatred. You have no right to make demands, or to place conditions, on the person who hurt you. You have no right to determine what that person will do with your offer of forgiveness.

I know a woman who was sexually abused by her father as a child. The abuse had a long-standing negative impact on the entire family. Following years of counseling and therapy, the woman developed a plan and a script (a victim impact statement) with which to approach her father. She did this to confront the pain and horror that she had experienced. More important, she needed to do it for her own well-being.

The father listened quietly, then stood and walked out.

He admitted no responsibility. He didn't acknowledge his daughter's comments, nor offer amends for his behavior. Years of abuse, manipulation and deceit had no doubt calloused his heart to the reality of his deplorable, dysfunctional behavior. The woman was shocked and disappointed, but her therapist had wisely prepared her for this possibility. Had she not been well prepared, she could have felt re-victimized. Instead, she felt a huge burden lifting from her shoulders. Because of her extraordinary courage, she felt that at last she could move on.

Your circumstances, your pain and your journey may be different from mine, and different from any that I've described. The principles still apply. Forgiveness works—it heals, and it changes lives. In fact, forgiveness is the only way to heal.

The only way you will find freedom and peace in hurtful situations is through the mystery and miracle of forgiveness. Forgiveness is a choice of the will, it is not a feeling. I invite you to make that choice. Accept forgiveness for yourself, and choose to feel the miracle in your life.

EXPLORATION

1. What is holding you back from forgiving those who hurt you?

2. What can you do to help you move on?
   Start by completing the following exercise:

   • Who hurt you?

   • How were you hurt? (neglect, verbal abuse, rejection, misunderstanding, betrayal, lies, desertion, sexual abuse, physical abuse, rape, etc)

   • How do you feel about that person?
     (Be honest—God knows exactly how you feel.)

   • Make a choice to forgive. Place a sheet of paper on a table as if placing it before God. Begin by confessing your unforgiveness.

   • Write out this prayer:

     God, I confess my unforgiveness of (name the person) for the (name the hurt) I experienced. I no longer want to hold onto the pain and resentment that I feel.

     I choose to forgive (name the person). I am placing (name) in your hands. I pray that you will heal me, and the wounds I have suffered. I am unlocking the handcuffs that bind me to (name the person).

     Amen.

   Now destroy that paper. Burn it, bury it, rip it to shreds, throw it in a river or scatter it in the wind. Choose any method that is meaningful to you. The important thing is to release the name and its contents to God.
   When you do all this, you will undoubtedly experience a sense of peace, release and freedom. Walk away.
   Be grateful it is over.

PRAYER

O God:

It has been such a long journey and I have carried this burden of unforgiveness for so long. I don't want to carry it anymore. I don't want to be a prisoner of the past. I want to be free to enjoy life. I believe you are able to free me from the past, from the person who hurt me, and from the hurts that have surrounded me. I want to be free to be all that you have intended me to be.

I have placed (name the person) in your hands. Now I am giving you my heart and my situation so that you can heal me and make something meaningful from all that I have experienced. The most important thing I need is your peace and your freedom.

I am also accepting your forgiveness of me for all the things I have done to hurt others. Thank you for your forgiveness of me and my unwillingness to let go and forgive others. Thank you for helping me find a way to heal. I am truly grateful for the gift of freedom and peace you have promised.

Amen.

HEALING:
The impact continues

AFTER SEVERAL MONTHS interacting with lifers in prisons and in Life-Line meetings, I was once again invited to travel to Richmond, Virginia to present a Victim Impact Statement. This time was for the sentencing of James Scruggs, the young man who carried the gun to the crime scene the night Soren was killed.

Only Soren's wife Starli, his daughter Niki, and I were invited to attend. To prepare, Clay and I shared our plans with a group of lifers we had been meeting with monthly. A special bond of trust had developed between us during those meetings. One lifer stood up and said, "On behalf of the whole group, we want you to know how important you and Clay have become to all of us. We want you to know that we will be thinking about you and praying for you as you speak in the courtroom."

What an unlikely group of supporters! I will forever treasure their thoughts and kind gestures as they approached me one by one to extend their personal best wishes.

Starli, Niki and I stayed at the same hotel in Virginia. The night before the sentencing we had a wonderful opportunity to talk. Those discussions were healing—we were each at different points in the healing process, but we accepted the unique ways in which we were individually progressing through the painful adjustments to Soren's death. We met once again with the federal prosecutor and the lead FBI agent. They advised us that a large group of family members and a church pastor would be present to support James. They warned us that as the judge handed down the sentence the emotional outbursts could be disruptive.

Starli would present her statement first. Niki would follow and I would be the last to speak. "I think you should be aware that at the conclusion of my statement I will be offering forgiveness to James Scruggs," I told them. The prosecutor seemed shocked, and one of the investigators replied, "You can't do that!" Amazed at his comment, I retorted in defiance, "My statement is my statement, and no one can stop me from saying what I have to say."

The room fell silent as we absorbed the interaction that had just occurred. The prosecutor started to speak, but became emotional and was unable to comment. We sat quietly for a few moments. He tried again, but was again too emotional to proceed. The FBI agent, sensitive to what was happening, took over the discussion. After a time, the prosecutor recovered his composure. "I was in Vietnam," he said. "Soren was a Vietnam war veteran as well. He came back a hero."

"Yes," I replied. "He came back a hero, but he too needed forgiveness and release from the things he did in Vietnam. He would never have done those things had he not been facing an enemy, and I'm sure those things plagued him till his dying day, but I believe God has forgiven him."

After leaving the conference room we were introduced to two FBI agents, a man and a woman. Relatively new to the force, they were former Black Hawk helicopter pilots in Vietnam. They had been told to attend this courtroom session, even though they had not been involved in Soren's case. They sat near us, making us feel secure and protected from the large family that was arriving. James was a handsome young man with a beautiful smile that he frequently flashed to his family. It was obvious that he was a cherished male who was gaining strength from the large contingent of females filling his side of the room. Some of the women may have been from a local church. The church pastor seemed to be the only male.

When it came time for our victim impact statements, Starli and Niki carefully and articulately described the despair and devastation Soren's death had caused. I'll never forget Niki's heartfelt tears as she described how her children would never grow to know the grandfather who loved them so much.

I approached the witness stand, resolute and comfortable with what I was about to say. My statement was similar to the one I presented at the sentencing of Travis, except that I focused on the choices James had made, and how different choices could have changed the outcome on that fateful night.

VICTIM IMPACT STATEMENT (excerpts)
Annette Stanwick

Accused:

James Scruggs
3 February 2003
Richmond, Virginia

When we learned that Soren's life had been taken on March 1, 1999, the thoughts of his murder created the most unbearable anguish and pain, and an agonizing sensation like my heart was being ripped out of my body, along with an overwhelming sense of grief and deep, deep sorrow. It is unbelievable that Soren could endure and withstand the danger and horridness of the Vietnam war, with friends and comrades dying all around him, only to succumb to the brutality of four fellow citizens intent on taking his life.

James, you intentionally brought your gun to the place where my brother's truck was parked. In your hands, you not only carried that gun, but you also carried the most incredible power of your own choice. You had the choice to walk away and to take your gun with you, or to even discard your gun so no one else could use it. If you had used the power of your choice, you could have changed the entire circumstances of what happened that night, and my brother just might be alive today.

James, in that one cowardly act, when you chose to hand your gun to Travis, you put in motion the use of that deadly weapon.

By your choice, you thrust my entire family into the middle of a murder mystery.

I described the impact of Soren's death on our family, and concluded with the following comments:

James, in spite of the unspeakable pain and sorrow of the past four years, that can never be fully described in these few statements, there are some very important things I have learned that have impacted me greatly.

Through God's goodness and his unconditional love and forgiveness, I am now able to look at you through eyes that see beyond the horrible thing you did in choosing to provide the gun that killed my brother.

What I am about to say will never excuse or erase what you did that night, and it will never diminish the need for justice, nor will it reduce the consequences of your actions. What I am about to say, however, does come from the very depths of my heart, after long hours of tearful prayer and deep contemplation.

James, I want you to know that through this whole incredible experience, my God has given me a new understanding of love and forgiveness.

God has impressed me that:

* Wrong will always be wrong, and he doesn't love what you did, but he has impressed me that he loves you in spite of what you did.

* He loves you just as much as he loves me and just as much as he loves my brother Soren.

* There is nothing so deep, so dark and so horrible that he cannot and will not forgive.

Here in this courtroom, I am offering you the gift of God's love and forgiveness and James, I am also offering you my forgiveness. Love and forgiveness will never change what has happened, and will never change the facts and the consequences of what you have done.

Through forgiveness, I have chosen to rise above this hideous thing that happened, but I will forever be sad that my brother's life was senselessly snuffed out and we cannot be with him or talk to him.

My forgiveness of you means that I have personally chosen to let go of my anger and my need for revenge and to let go of the bitterness and hatred that once bound and chained my heart and life.

It may be hard for you to understand, but I now hold no bitterness toward you for this horrible act. I only hold a deep, deep sadness for the decisions you made, and the incredible consequences of your decisions. As a result of Soren's death and my own need for healing, God has transformed my heart in ways I never thought could be possible.

As hard as it is to believe, I now see murderers as God's children. I now have a burden to help murderers understand what they have done, and to help them understand how much God loves them in spite of what they have done. The mystery is how God's love can use the wretchedness of my brother's death to impact and change not only my heart and life, but also the lives and hearts of murderers inside prison walls, as well as others touched by this message of forgiveness.

I pray that you too can be changed by what you've heard today. I will be praying for you, that as you sit in your cell, you will acknowledge the truth of what you have done and that you will take full responsibility for your own actions in this horrible picture. I pray that you will make every effort to change your life. If you allow him, God can heal your heart and he is willing to help you change your life.

James, by your choice, you have forever impacted the lives of our family. I am now pleading with you and will be praying that you will make choices that will allow God's healing love to make an impact in your life that can affect you for eternity.

After I sat down, James Scruggs stood and looked at his family. Then he looked directly at me. He said, "I didn't have anything to do with Mr. Cornforth's death but, Mrs. Stanwick, I am so thankful for the comments you made. I will carry your thoughts with me for the rest of my life."

I knew that he didn't actually take Soren's life, and that he couldn't admit to anything in the presence of so large a crowd of adoring women. I was moved that he acknowledged what I had said was a great gift. I believe my message of love and forgiveness had made its mark. I felt deep compassion for him despite his personal choice to carry the gun that had made Soren's death possible.

Bedlam erupted when the judge issued James a life sentence. His mother, sisters, aunts and other women started crying, shouting and moaning. We were grateful for the presence of the FBI agents who cloistered themselves around us until the chaos settled. Afterward, the former helicopter pilots came to me privately and said, "Annette, now we know why we were directed to attend this session today. We needed to hear every word you said." The lead FBI agent said, "Annette, no one would ever try to stop you from saying the things you said."

The forensic pathologist said, "We didn't know what you were going to say next. I didn't want to miss a word or even a syllable of what you had to say."

In his office later, the prosecutor showed me a picture. In it was his former wife, with whom he must share custody of his beautiful children. I could sense his sadness that his marriage had collapsed. I was almost overcome with emotion when he, too, said, "I needed to hear everything you had to say today."

As Niki and I boarded the plane, the flight attendant greeted us. "Someone has arranged for you to fly first class," he said, refusing to disclose the name of the person.

I couldn't believe how soft the landing was in Texas. As we stood to disembark, the pilot appeared and I shook his hand, saying, "Thank you for the most beautiful landing I have ever experienced in all my travels. It was like landing on a cloud." "That landing was for you," he responded. "We know what you've just come through, and you deserve something special."

The Prayer of Jabez, by Bruce Wilkinson, had been a precious book to me in the months after I came to the point of forgiveness. In that book, Wilkinson talks about God expanding one's territory. As I delivered my message of forgiveness in federal prisons and other places prior to going to Virginia, I had been praying that God would expand my own territory for his message of forgiveness. On that trip over a three-day period I had sixteen encounters—ranging from taxi drivers, lawyers, FBI agents, courtroom marshals, an aeronautical engineer, flight attendants and private citizens —where I knew without a doubt that the message of forgiveness had touched another person's heart.

God was truly expanding my territory, and his arrangements were beyond my imagination.

. . . .

FORGIVENESS:
Why it is possible

MANY TIMES I HAVE MENTIONED how God has moved in my life and throughout my journey of healing that led to forgiveness. I cannot bring this book to an end without briefly explaining how God accomplishes forgiveness.

Every person on earth has been separated from God our Creator because of sin. The wonderful intimate relationship our ancestors Adam and Eve had with God was shattered by their choice to disobey. As a result, the human race not only became separated from its Creator, but it also began to die. It is only a God of love that would create us with the freedom of choice in spite of the potential for a wrongful choice.

Because of the wonderful love God has for the entire human race, the plan of salvation was immediately activated. At precisely the right time, God sent his son Jesus Christ to our world as a helpless human baby. Jesus lived among the human race for more than thirty years. His life, his teachings and his miracles revealed the love and compassion of God the Father who longed to restore the relationship with us that had been broken.

The ultimate and incredible demonstration of love made by Jesus was his death. His death on the cross paid the penalty for the sins of the whole human race.

Through that unbelievable act, God the Father is able to offer forgiveness to every person who believes and accepts Jesus Christ as their Savior from sin, and acknowledges their need for forgiveness. *(John 3:16, 1John 1:9)*

Because of what Jesus Christ accomplished for us on the cross, we can be forgiven and restored to a wonderful and intimate relationship with God that will continue for eternity.

It is only because of God's grace and the death of Jesus Christ that I have been forgiven of my mistakes and have been restored to a wonderful relationship with him.

I have said a number of times, it is not because of my goodness that I was able to offer forgiveness to the individuals who took my brother's life. It was because I had experienced complete forgiveness, and because God had made it so very clear to me that he loved the men who took Soren's life. Jesus Christ's death on the cross paid the penalty for their sins as well as mine. *(Romans 10:9, 10)*

Jesus Christ is my hero, my Savior and my friend. It is only because of his love and presence in my life that I have experienced this incredible healing. He is the one who placed the passion in my heart to help others in their journey toward healing, wholeness and happiness.

PRAYER

If you would like to know and accept Jesus Christ as your personal Savior and friend, please pray the following prayer:

Dear God of Heaven and Earth:

I know I am a sinner and I need forgiveness. I believe your Son Jesus Christ died on the cross to pay the penalty for my sins. I accept Jesus as my Lord and Savior.

I invite you into my life and I open my heart to receive your unconditional love, acceptance and forgiveness. I desire to know you more fully and I want to experience your presence and power in my life. I thank you for your incredible gift of forgiveness and for loving me in spite of my past.

Amen.

WOUNDEDNESS:
How a community brings healing

WHEN A SERIOUS CRIME OCCURS, the impact of the offense is far reaching. The victim is injured and in this case he died. The victim's family, friends and community are wounded in ways that I could not fully describe in this book. The opportunity for our family to present victim impact statements was a tremendous means of opening the door to allow our wounded hearts to be heard.

On the other hand, the offender's family, friends and community are also wounded and left to struggle with the shame, guilt, mistrust and backlash caused by the actions of one of their own.

Families of offenders become victims as well. They too are plunged into a state of crisis. They are often punished, ostracized, stigmatized, and isolated either by their community or by their own shame at what has happened. In either case their wounds are deep and painful, and unless they are empowered to find a way to heal, they will remain wounded, isolated and afraid in spite of the fact that they too are in total shock and disbelief at the actions of their loved one. Family members of the offender also need someone to open the door so they too can be heard.

The community of the victim and the community of the offender suffer tremendously because of an offense. The community of the victim must deal with the loss and what that represents and how they are impacted. They often rally with support, tangible tokens of their compassion and ongoing encouragement that is so helpful to the family in distress. The value of those actions can never be fully appreciated or understood.

The community of the offender also experiences loss but in a totally different way. Their loss may be in reputation, safety, community pride and a whole host of other losses we often overlook. As a result of Soren's death, private citizens in the city of Richmond, Virginia were horrified at what had happened in their beautiful city. A news reporter wrote a meaningful article about Soren and who he was. Owners of the business where Soren's death occurred along with readers captivated by the story took action. They reached out to Soren's wife emotionally and financially to ease her plight even though they didn't know her and in spite of the great geographical distance. In making that connection and offering their compassion in tangible ways, a bridge of friendship developed that helped her and vicariously other family members as well.

In a further demonstration of their support, they attended the sentencing of Travis and later that of James. At the conclusion of those stressful events they invited our entire family into their private home providing unbelievably gracious hospitality in the midst of a city where hostile acts had ended Soren's life.

A retired police officer voluntarily chauffeured us around the city, to and from our hotel, obtaining newspapers that contained headlines of the courtroom scenes we had experienced. He also showed us a rose bush he had planted in his own yard in memory of Soren. An FBI agent and others toured us through the historic sites, helping us see the unmistakable beauty of the city that stood in stark contrast to the terrible deadliness that Soren had experienced.

Upon leaving Richmond, I purchased the book *Old Richmond Today* by Richard Cheek. The pictorial display captures the beauty of Richmond's grandeur.

A statement in the book reads, "To live in Richmond is a privilege, to visit a pleasure." What an enigma. Soren's visit to Richmond resulted in his death. I penned the following words in the front of the book:

"This book was purchased as a memory of the picture of compassion that the people of Richmond provided to my entire family surrounding the murder of my brother Soren in their fair city. The Department of Justice, the FBI, police officers, volunteers, media and private citizens were wonderful examples of people in community who reached out in professional, dignified and loving acts that brought compassion and healing to our world of pain."

The image of Richmond had been wounded, but people took action to help heal the wounds. By facing the painful situation, identifying what their community had lost and then stepping out in service to others, they helped to restore the dignity of their beloved city. Through those unselfish, courageous and compassionate endeavors they not only healed some of the wounds their community had suffered, but in doing so they helped bring healing to our wounded family.

What a wonderful model of community those citizens created by taking action despite having no responsibility for the adversity some of their own community members had created. Their acts truly demonstrated restorative justice in action. Our family will never forget the wonderful people of Richmond, Virginia.

RESOURCE GUIDE

T HE FOLLOWING IS A LIST of recommended reading and
seminars. All of the references mentioned in *Forgiveness:
The Mystery and Miracle* are included. (see asterisks)

RECOMMENDED READING

An Interpretive Inquiry Into Women's Experience of Adult Sibling Bereavement
by Susann M. Laverty. University of Calgary, Ph.D. Study,
Department of Psychology. 2001.

Becoming A Contagious Christian by Bill Hybels and Mark Mittelberg.
Grand Rapids, Michigan: Zondervan Publishing House, 1994.

★*Choices That Change Lives; 5 Ways To Find More Purpose, Meaning, And
Joy* by Hal Urban. New York, New York: Simon & Schuster, 2006.

★*Confronting The Horror; The Aftermath Of Violence* by Wilma L. Derksen.
Winnipeg, Manitoba: Amity Publishers, 2002.

★*Embracing Brokenness; How God Refines Us Through Life's Disappointments*
by Alan E. Nelson. Colorado Springs, Colorado: NavPress, 2002.

★*Feel The Fear And Do It Anyway* by Susan Jeffers, Ph.D. New York,
New York: Ballantine Books, 1987.

★*Forgive And Build Bridges; The Inner Strength Series. Living With Strength
In Today's World* by John Bevere. Lake Mary, Florida: Charisma
House a part of Strang Communications Company, 2002.

★*Forgive For Good; A Proven Prescription For Health And Happiness* by
Dr. Fred Luskin. New York, New York: HarperCollins
Publishers, Inc., 2002.

Forgiveness; The Greatest Healer of All by Gerald G. Jampolsky, M.D.

★*Gateway To Joy; Reflections That Draw Us Nearer To God* by Elisabeth Elliot, Ann Arbor, Michigan: Servant Publications, 1998.

★*How To Forgive When You Can't Forget; Healing Our Personal Relationships* by Charles Klein. Bellmore, New York: Liebling Press, Inc., 1995.

If You Want To Walk On Water, You've Got To Get Out Of The Boat by John Ortberg. Grand Rapids, Michigan: Zondervan Publishing House, 2001.

Just Walk Across The Room; Simple Steps Pointing People To Faith by Bill Hybels. Grand Rapids, Michigan: Zondervan Publishing House, 2006.

★*Life Strategies: Doing What Works; Doing What Matters* by Phillip C. McGraw, Ph.D. New York, New York: Hyperion, 1999.

★*Making Your Dreams Your Destiny; A Woman's Guide To Awakening Your Passions And Fulfilling Your Purpose* by Judy Rushfeldt. Kitchener, Ontario: Castle Quay Books, 2005.

★*Paper Doll; Lessons Learned From A Life Lived In The Headlines* by LuAn Mitchell-Halter. San Diego, California: Jodere Group, Inc., 2003.

★*Prayer; Finding The Heart's True Home* by Richard J. Foster. New York, New York: Harper Collins Publishers, 1992.

★*Self Matters; Creating Your Life From The Inside Out* by Phillip C. McGraw, Ph.D. New York, New York: Simon & Schuster, Inc., 2001.

★*Social Intelligence; The New Science Of Human Relationships* by Daniel Goleman. New York, New York: Bantom Dell, 2006.

★*The Art Of Forgiving: When You Need To Forgive And Don't Know How* by Lewis B. Smedes. New York, New York: Ballantine Books, 1996.

The Divine Embrace; An Invitation To The Dance Of Intimacy With Christ. One Exhilarating Ennobling, Uncertain Step At A Time by Ken Gire. Colorado Springs, Colorado: Alive Communications, Inc., 2003.

★*The Forgiveness Prescription; Get Rapid Relief from Fears, Anger, and Resentment* by Alice Wheaton. Calgary, Alberta: CoreGowth Foundations Inc. Publishers, 2007

★*The Freedom Of Forgiveness* by David Augsburger. Chicago, Illinois: Moody Press, 1970, 1988.

The Healthy CEO; Taking The Lead In Your Physical, Relational And Financial Wellness by Dr. Larry Ohlhauser, M.D. Edmonton, Alberta: June Warren Publishing, Ltd., 2007.

The Nature Of Success by Mac Anderson. Nashville, Tennessee: J. Countryman, Division of The Thomas Nelson Book Group, 2003.

★*The Power Of Attitude* by Mac Anderson. Nashville, Tennessee: J. Countryman, Division of The Thomas Nelson Book Group, 2004.

★*The Power Of Focus; How To Hit Your Business, Personal And Financial Targets With Absolute Certainty* by Jack Canfield, Mark Victor Hansen and Les Hewitt. Deerfield Beach, Florida: Health Communications, Inc., 2000.

★*The Power Of Focus For Women; How To Live The Life You Really Want* by Fran Hewitt and Les Hewitt. Deerfield Beach, Florida: Health Communications, Inc., 2003.

★*The Prayer Of Jabez Devotional; Thirty-One Days To Experiencing More Of The Blessed Life* by Bruce Wilkinson. Sisters, Oregon: Multnomah Publishers, Inc., 2001.

★*The Purpose Driven Life; What On Earth Am I Here For* by Rick Warren. Grand Rapids, Michigan: Zondervan Publishing House, 2002.

The Road To Forgiveness; Hearts Shattered By Tragedy, Transformed By Love by Bill and Cindy Griffiths. Nashville, Tennessee: Thomas Nelson, Inc., 2001.

The Success Principles; How To Get From Where You Are To Where You Want To Be by Jack Canfield. New York, New York: Harper Collins Publishers Inc., 2005.

★*What About The Big Stuff?; Finding Strength And Moving Forward When The Stakes Are High* by Richard Carlson, Ph.D. New York, New York: Hyperion, 2002.

★*Your Scars Are Beautiful To God; Finding Peace And Purpose In The Hurts Of Your Past* by Sharon Jaynes. Eugene, Oregon: Harvest House Publishers, 2006.

SEMINARS

CHOICES Seminars: Changing The World One Heart At a Time: www.CHOICESintl.com

WE WOULD APPRECIATE RECEIVING YOUR FEEDBACK REGARDING THIS BOOK.

Please send your comments to:

www.comments@annettestanwick.com

ANNETTE STANWICK

is available for

KEYNOTES, SEMINARS, RETREATS
AND WORKSHOPS

that

INSPIRE, MOTIVATE AND UPLIFT

Individuals, Groups and Organizations
in their quest for

Passion, Purpose, Freedom and Peace.

HEART MESSAGE
PRODUCTIONS

TO BOOK ANNETTE

To speak or facilitate at your conference or event

VISIT

www.annettestanwick.com
E-mail: info@annettestanwick.com
Phone: 403-**208-2181**

ABOUT THE AUTHOR

ANNETTE STANWICK has a Bachelor of Science in Nursing and more than twenty five years experience at a senior level in nursing, nursing education and hospital administration in small and large hospitals across Canada. For several years she owned and operated her own management and motivation consulting business. She then moved into executive health care management in private health care. Over the years she has served on numerous professional committees, boards, advisory committees, and has held leadership positions in various churches and other volunteer organizations.

Annette Stanwick is a captivating speaker who has challenged, inspired and motivated audiences across North America. Her passionate, lively and life changing messages have touched women's groups, university students, professionals and organizational leaders inspiring them to look deeper and climb higher in their search for passion, purpose, fulfillment, joy and peace in their lives.

Drawing on years of experience in executive management along with deep personal challenges in her own life, coupled with a passion to encourage and uplift others, Annette brings a dynamic enthusiasm to her diverse keynotes, seminars and workshops.

Her values, experience, deep learnings and communication style help her audiences see the world through a new set of eyes, helping individuals find new ways of relating to life and relationships; giving them courage to rise above life's obstacles, to find deep meaning in the midst of stress and turmoil, moving on to be the best they can be.

Annette brings balance to her busy life by engaging in numerous creative pursuits, riding her motorcycle, and enjoying the thrill of life with her husband, two daughters and their families.

....

WE need to learn to forgive.

How do we learn to forgive?

By knowing we too need to be forgiven.

—Mother Theresa